Occupy The World!

From the Heart of the Protesters

By Hannah Faye

Copyright © 2011 by Hannah Faye

Be sure to visit arapperscollege.weebly.com for more information and to connect with Hannah Faye.

TO THE READER

To explore the true history of protests and demonstrations one would have to examine human history and find evidence to support when exactly minds began to think for themselves. One would have to explore when the perception for right and wrong became different amongst minds and how they began to influence each other. To find the beginning of protests and demonstrations is to find the beginning of when humans first began to figure out how and when it is appropriate to take a stand for what they believe in. With that being said, it is nearly impossible to number and document the protests and demonstrations that have happened throughout world history and perhaps even those happening right now. For as long as the human mind is able to think for itself, there will always be a cause for revolution. In fact, protests should be nothing new to any human being; for they have been a significant part of our lives whether we choose to be apart of them or not.

Earlier in 2011 the meeting of several minds resulted in protests all over the world, specifically in Israel, Egypt and Spain. None of the protests were broadcasted in the U.S. quite as much as the one which took place in Egypt, led by ordinary people dissatisfied with their government. Perhaps, the world expected it to just be another protest that would soon disintegrate like all the rest without any of the demands of protesters being met, however surprisingly, most of the world watched as the persistence of the demonstrators finally led to the Egyptian President's resignation. It was a true victory for them indeed and perhaps also a victory for people across the world; for those who inwardly hold bitterness toward their own governments. And just a few months after the Egyptian victory, a few days after the anniversary of the catastrophes which took place on 9/11, the energy which fueled Egyptian protesters has now prompted the rest of the world to action, even reaching to the borders of the United States.

In the U.S. the protesters have made themselves known by their demonstrations. They've given themselves a name. They are called the word *Occupy* followed by the name of the city, town or street in which they choose to assemble. According to the website, the protesters were first referred to as *Occupy Wall Street* by a group called *Adbusters* on July 13, 2011. Visit the general website, *occupywallst.org* and you'll find more information about where and how the protesting began. To summarize, what began in Egypt has now made its way across the world, reaching the U.S., beginning in New York City's financial district, Wall Street and has now spread throughout the country.

As for the protesters themselves, you won't find very much information about them on the website. The information about the actual participants remains a bit vague. After the original protesters were given the title *Occupy Wall Street* the New York group claims it was then they formed a "planning group" and established a web page. Although they declare to have no leader many critics believe they do. In fact, some who oppose the *Occupy Wall Street* idea claim it is not authentic at all and that unknown billionaires sit behind closed doors orchestrating it all. However, after going through the testimonies again throughout this book, I find that hard to believe. In any case, if these "unknown billionaires" did in fact start this whole thing they will certainly not be able to predict how it will all end; for in the protesters own words they are: "A people-powered movement that began on September 17, 2011 in Liberty Square in Manhattan's Financial District, and have spread to over 100 cities in the United States and actions in over 1,500 cities globally." In my opinion, these so called "unknown billionaires" would have to be some extraordinary persons to influence such a global reaction in such a short amount of time.

In any case, the author has somewhat of a bone to pick with *Occupy Wall Street*. Perhaps it may be viewed as a small bone, but I feel it is one that may possibly alter the course of history. I wish to clarify the quote made above. The fact is that protests now happening across the world did not begin on Wall Street, but in Egypt (See quote above). Simply put *Occupy Wall Street* is a part of a much larger movement of protests which were already taking place worldwide. *Occupy Wall Street* is a group of protesters from New York City, who simply began demonstrations in America. As a result, we now have *Occupy Chicago, Occupy Los Angeles, Occupy Atlanta, etc.* Now, whether or not other countries saw what was going on here in the U.S. and decided to follow suit is questionable. However, there should be absolutely no doubt that protesters all over the world are

4

influenced by what happened in Africa (Egypt), maybe not in *how* they were protesting, but in the persistence to achieve a desired result. *Occupy Wall Street* must not lose its integrity by ignoring the source of their beginnings and the fact they were: "inspired by the uprisings in Egypt and Tunisia." We must not slip into the error of taking other's ideas and calling them our own.

Aside from the fact that some protesters around the world may be a bit confused about the movement's origination and maintenance, they are sure of this one thing: they are an affinity group; a group of ordinary people from different parts of the world, who have united for similar causes, which range from issues with healthcare to issues with school systems to issues with marriage, poverty, the class system, food, social security, war, unemployment, taxes, and the list goes on and on. The concerns depend on what part of the world the individual protesters live in and what is important to the people living in that area. This is why the protests are so significant to world history, because they are bringing people together who are thousands of miles away from each other who don't have a damn thing in common with one another except for the fact that they are human beings and they know what is wrong should be made right!

But there's something missing in all the hype. For all the people with all their issues in different countries, there seems to be no protester or group of protesters with a clear strategy on exactly how the issues should be solved or who exactly to direct their concerns to. The protesters must find a way to unite amongst themselves if they are to achieve any results. They have been collectively blaming "the rich" or "the government officials." Protesters in the U.S. say they are: "Fighting back against corrosive power of major banks and multinational corporations over the democratic process, and the role of Wall Street in creating an economic collapse that has caused the greatest recession in generations. The movement...aims to expose how the richest 1% of people are writing the rules of an unfair global economy that is foreclosing on our future." So even though the protesters are not specifying who exactly to go after to solve their issues, those who have the power to solve them know the protesters are speaking about them! These unspecified people...and they know who they are, know they have the power to make the changes, but because they are not being called out specifically, they feel they are somewhat "safe." Up to this point, participants of the *Occupy Movement* haven't blamed any specific individuals. The majority have only mentioned a general rich "1%." But who are the 1%? And what happens when or if the protesters begin calling them out? What happens if the protesters begin calling out the names of individual corporations and big businesses such as Wal-Mart, McDonald's, even though they've handed out free coffee to protesters, ATT, Sprite, Nike, Comcast and Ford Motor Company? What if the protesters begin going after corporate spokesmen and the innumerable celebrities that represent them? What if the protesters begin blaming the rich specifically; people like Warren Buffet, Donald Trump, Oprah Winfrey or Bill Gates, politicians like the Doberman Pinscher of Chicago, Rahm Emanuel, other government officials, judges, lawyers, doctors, innumerable celebrities, overpaid athletes, entertainers, and rap artists like Snoop Dog who are allowed to profit millions of dollars each year off of promoting booty shaking and weed...what a legacy to leave behind by the way, along with all the other rich people who like to boast of their prosperity? And is it me or have our most favorite entertainers been extremely quiet about the *Occupy Movement* issue? Correct me if I'm wrong, but it doesn't seem like many of them have had anything to say about it. Could it be because they've been instructed not to? Or maybe it's because they are apart of the 1% themselves. Surely they wouldn't protest against themselves. Lucky for them, the *Occupy Movement* doesn't seem to be blaming any one specifically. For now, they are using: "A tool known as 'people's assembly' to facilitate collective decision making in an open, participatory and non-binding manner." They are a diverse group of people who say: "We welcome people from all colors, genders and beliefs to attend our daily assemblies." Referring to themselves as "the 99%" they say they will: "Fight back against social injustice" and they are more than willing to face the consequences.

As expressed above, the demographics of the movement include all people. Most recently an editor of a Chicago newspaper, who shall remain unnamed, included a column from an outsider who concluded ignorantly that the movement was led by a group of young hippies that, and I quote: "Need to go back to living in their parents' basements." To clarify, the protesters come from all walks of life.

They are young and they are old. In the U.S. they are African-American, European-American, Chinese-American, Latin-American, Arab-American, etc. They are women, men, and people of all ages, all religious beliefs and Atheists. They are republicans and they are democrats. They are wealthy and they are in poverty. They are strong, but some of them are weak. They are scholars and they are uneducated. They are straight and they are homosexuals. They are liberals and independents. They are communists and they are capitalists, mobilizing in groups ranging from a couple hundred to thousands of people.

Speaking of capitalists, as you may or may not imagine a group of this size composed of such diversity can easily be turned into a hot spot for potential business. Those who seek to capitalize off of people's sincerity are already at work, seeking to make money off the event by producing T-shirts, hats, and other souvenirs and memorabilia to go along with the event while many have started websites and individual accounts with social networks. Personally, I'm waiting for an official, national donating center to open up if it hasn't already to fund this event. I expect the funds to all of a sudden come up missing soon after they are collected. I know what you're thinking. You're probably forming the opinion that I'm no different from them, capitalizing off of the event myself by writing this book and selling it, right? However it might settle you to know that all my books are free. All you have to do is ask. And years from now when the movie is being made about the event that sparked a worldwide revolution, I doubt theatres will forget to charge you for your temporary entry. And might I add, rarely will you find good books free from an author such as my self...wink, wink.

The only regret I have is that unfortunately, I was only able to visit Chicago, Illinois and New York to obtain testimonies from protesters for book inclusion. I wish I could've traveled the world over and interviewed people for optimal diversity. I haven't bothered to list the races, sexes and religious beliefs of my interviewees, but I can assure you they were quite a diverse group, composed of people who weren't from all over the globe, but were more importantly global thinkers and you can feel it in their responses. The 26 interviewees were not paid for their testimonies and therefore the opinions and ideas expressed remain untapped. They were given a choice as to whether or not they wanted to write their testimonies or have them recorded. The testimonies are only slightly edited for reader's comprehension. The author's goal was to maintain the authentic speech for each individual protester; therefore the testimonies were transcribed word-for-word as much as possible. All participants were asked to answer one general question: Why are you a participant in the *Occupy Movement* which is now spreading throughout the world? Now, I present to you their answers in *Occupy the World: From the Heart of the Protesters*, the first book of documented testimonies of protesters.

"The Revolution will not be televised....it is not an event, but a process." -Professor Griff, Public Enemy

WARNING

What you are about to read has not been approved by any corporation. It is not a professionally written manuscript designed for professional readers. Instead it is written for the people by the people. The author does not expect it to be recorded or reviewed by such reviewers as the New York Times partly because the author believes they themselves need to be occupied for their discrimination. This book is self-published because the author has been rejected by main stream publishing companies. And what was once viewed as a discouragement has most recently become an encouragement, due to the fact that the author now understands how publishing companies work. They are like Hollywood. Most of their business is driven by what sales instead of the desire to educate and enlighten. Publishing companies need to be overhauled and reconstructed, especially the bloodsucking ones who are eager to follow the example of *Publish America*. The author will not be interviewed because she is in favor of an *Occupy Media*. Everything that needs to be said has already been said here, within these pages. There are no more questions to be answered. The people's protest is my protest. This is my protest.

Occupy Chicago 2011

1

Nick, 21

Date: Monday, October 24, 2011
Location: Between Jackson & LaSalle Street, Chicago, IL
Event: Occupy Chicago
Occupation: Student, Stocker
Transcribed Voice Recording

My name is Nick Poletta. I'm definitely an active participant. I'm not one of the core members that stay out here every single night but I'm here almost every single day. I'm 21 years old. I'm not originally from Chicago. I'm from the Chicago-land suburbs, a town called Joliet. It's more of a city. I've actually been living up here (in Chicago) for school about over a year. Very simply, the reason why I'm here is because I've been waiting for this movement to happen for a long time. I've been waiting for this movement to happen for a while. It's because I've known something like this was going to happen. This was inevitable. I'm not just a member of the movement here, but I'm also a member of what's called the *Zeitgeist Movement*. The Zeitgeist Movement is a social awareness movement to educate the public towards the idea of moving towards a research based economy. I'll explain more about that later. The main idea is that the social system we (all people) exist in now is not necessarily a democracy, it's not necessarily socialism or communism; and this goes for any other country in the world. It's not so much any of that, but that we all exist in a monetary paradigm. The monetary paradigm is basically the foundational structure of our civilization as we know it right now. The monetary structure is used by any society that chooses to use money in exchange for services, goods, products, etc. So that obviously describes us (U.S.). Some people call it specifically capitalism, some people call it neo-capitalism, that (term) is more modernized, but it all describes a monetary system. This monetary paradigm as we know it, as unfortunate as it is, is collapsing as we speak. Now the reason why I say this is because this is obviously apparent any where you look if you take the time to look around the world today. Monetary systems in any past civilization over the course of human history have always failed. Monetary structures do not last because they have some very fundamental flaws that do not allow them to exist longer than a certain period. That isn't to say that monetary structures are not good in their own specific ways. They're just unsustainable overall. As far as the monetary structure goes, the capitalist system that we have now, when we talk about representing the 99%, we talk about representing the vast majority of people who this system does not sustain; (the people) this system does not want to sustain. This system is basically set up to sustain 1% or less of the population, which in this system is the extremely wealthy class and people who just have money, like the owners of banks and stuff like that. So, at this point as far as the movement goes we're actually waking up to this paradigm (and realizing) this entire system does not sustain us, not just for living but when it comes to accessing food, accessing healthcare, accessing education...these things are not being provided for us and are not being taken care of. And even if they are provided for us the one thing that we cannot escape from in this system is the monetary debt. Debt is the foundation of this entire society. In this society money is debt and debt is money. There's no two ways around it. So when thinking about this, every single dollar that you have in your pocket right now is owed by someone to someone else. Now, this may not seem like a big problem to some people as it is to other people because some people will say: "Okay, I have enough money, even if I pay off all my debts I'll still have money left over." Well the money itself was created out of debt in the first place. And that's a very, very fundamental flaw within the system. A lot of people say that factories or banking is the problem. The Federal Reserve of the United States is also a problem and the fact that they print money out of nothing. It's (the money) backed by absolutely nothing. It's just green paper with writing on it. Although that is a problem within itself the very fact that the money even exists in the first place is the root problem. That is the founding problem. Now, I'm not going to sit here and say that I'm necessarily a religious person. I'm not going to tell you that money is the root of all evil or that money is evil. It's not the fact that the money is evil. It's the fact that society itself is unsustainable as long as it uses money. So it goes beyond any good verses evil. This isn't about that. So basically, in regards to this movement specifically, the movement is more of a coalition effort at this point between multiple groups. There are capitalists here. There are socialists here. There are communists. There are lots and lots of people here. But there are also representatives and members of the Zeitgeist Movement, like myself and a few other people here. Many, many people have seen the Zeitgeist movie on (social video network). They've downloaded it. At a lot of events, all around the world we actually give out the DVDs free to people. The most recent (movie) *Zeitgeist: Moving Forward* is probably the best documentary that has come out within the past few decades. Basically, it explains the social paradigm we all live in. We're finally waking up to the idea that this system will collapse. It will not work. When we look at, not just the United States, but countries like Greece, Rome and Italy, especially on the 15th last week, there are riots happening everywhere, all around the world. We cannot ignore these things. We can't just say: "Oh, well we're going to use this movement so that the middle working class here in America has a better life." No, that shouldn't be the end goal. We're (protesters) not as self-centered as people think. A person like me doesn't just look locally or nationally. I look globally toward all people. We need a system that sustains all people on this planet. The resource based economic model, after years of researching it myself is how I arrived at this conclusion. It is the decision I arrived at. This is the thing that makes the most sense. It (the Resource Based Economic Model) is not based on scientific evidence or any one person's opinion, but is based on empirical data and objectivity. It's based on the natural laws of the universe, things that no human is exempt from. It's based on the idea that we have certain human needs to fulfill. If these needs are not met than it leads to deprivation, mental health issues, heart issues, and health issues in general. It also leads to problems with inferiority, the class system, structural racism, which are all foundations of this society as well. In the future, all these things will be looked down upon if any person engages in any of them. If a person says: "My life matters more than your life" only because of their own subjective notion they're not going to matter much at all. I'd also like to say in general there are age old notions; there are religious notions and personal opinions that claim there are fundamental flaws with human beings. Ones that say humans are naturally greedy, corrupt and that we have infinite desires for more than what we need. I'm sorry to say, but modern science, in this day and age proves that these ideas are completely wrong. It's absolutely impossible that a person can grow up and be naturally greedy in any social system. It is true that in this American, democratic system that a person can be conditioned to believe that these notions are true without any empirical data. People are just told these ideas are true without any evidence. Again, I'm sorry to say but I'm here to tell people there's nothing wrong with human beings whatsoever. Human beings are basically born with blank slates. And what conditions us, the biggest factor for us is the environment itself. A person who grows up in a capitalist system will become a capitalist. There's no two ways around it. A person who grows up in a egalitarian society will chose to value family more, value their tribe more, they may even grow up with the notion that property ownership doesn't even really exist, but that everything is to be shared between persons. Age old notions about the existence of fundamental flaws within human beings are impossible. Also when any person says that human beings are just naturally corrupt and we are just naturally evil I'm sorry but that person is going to have to take a good, hard look at them selves and say: "There must be a problem with me as well. I must be corrupt. There must be some fundamental flaw with me as well." But I don't think any person wants to do that. I don't think any person wants to say they have a problem. Well, the truth is there isn't a problem. There isn't anything wrong with us (humans) at all. We just have to wake up and realize that the structural problems we have today are not subjective. They are not personal problems with human beings. The larger problem is the entire social system itself. It's outdated, un-functional, and unsustainable. It will not sustain every human being forever. We're at the point where our entire country is not able to sustain anymore. We're going to war to steal resources. I mean, you hear people talking about World War Three! If it happens it's just going to be a grab for resources. We've been invading other countries because they have oil. They have water. But these are things people need within their own countries to be able to survive. We have to wake up and realize that all resources are a common heritage to all people who live on this planet. One person cannot sit there and say: "This spot of land, this bit of food, this is mine." No, it's a share between all people. Sharing is going to be the key in the future. We have enough that we can share all the resources on this planet. It's more than enough for everyone. In a finite system, we need global sustainability...not local, not national, but global. We need all people to be participants in a system which literally sustains all human beings.

2

Austin, 31

Date: Monday, October 24, 2011
Location: Between Jackson & LaSalle Street, Chicago, IL
Event: Occupy Chicago
Occupation: Stylist, D.J., Activist
Written Response

When Austin Enriquez, 31 was asked why he chose to participate in the Occupy Movement which is now spreading throughout the world, he chose to answer in a thoughtful, handwritten response:

I'm actually here for a different cause altogether. I see this event to be the start of something amazing, something never before seen...ever. It is my goal to help educate and possibly guide a mind set out of its current frame and into or onto a path more inclusive of natural law. All life needs clean water, air and nutrition to sustain itself and the life around it. Many signs read something to the effect of: "End the FED" as though this would create any change. Is there any doubt that by doing so would simply put in its place yet another central bank of this sort? You may see signs that address money in politics and that it must be removed but isn't the political system itself a part of the issue? By helping to focus people's attention on underlying causes and away from the surface effects we can then hope to see the start of true change. There is a strong focus on a 1% here and where I see some understanding that this division is false, many do not. Slowly, however the crowd is changing. This 1% is greed and violence, not an individual or group. And as this understanding is embraced by one world and one people, the focus will shift, and generations to come will be able to inherit a peaceful planet.

3

Winifred, 71

Date: Monday, October 24, 2011
Location: Between Jackson & LaSalle Street, Chicago, IL
Event: Occupy Chicago
Occupation: Librarian Page
Transcribed Voice Recording

I'm Winifred Thivel. I'm a third generation Chicagoan. I'm here because I believe in this. These bankers fooled us twice. They never used the money as they were supposed to. They just put it away for safekeeping. And there are so many people who are losing their jobs. Money seems to be their (bankers) life. They think if they can reduce us all to ants on a hill than that's what we're on this planet for. You have to realize, I thought they were going to use this money to educate and give diplomas out to people, but I guess an educated person would be a threat to them. People are individuals. Each person has something to give. And it shouldn't be up to Wall Street to decide when to reduce people to ants. I am going to fight for this. I came today to bare witness. I'll be joining other protests. On November 11, 2011 I'm going to come down for the Jane Adam's protest. I know there's going to be quite a few of us to protest the fact that they (the government) would dare go after the middle class and the poor. I mean, we have every right to live a decent life and just because they (the banks) had a step up one way or another doesn't mean that their contribution is more than ours. Unless we educate people we're never going to know what their talent was or what their gift was. This is the way human beings are developed...by communication and setting an example. We can't let somebody tell us we can't do certain things. We all have just a much right as anybody else. And that's what this is about. Our rights are being trampled on and they are trying to reduce us to nothing. You know, we were the ones that helped them. We elect these people and what do they do? They turn around and accept money and some other advantages from a person who's in power at the time. That's not what they're sent for. They're supposed to be representing us. I think there is a very serious revolution coming. Democracies only last about 200 years. It is an ideal, but it's what you do with it. They have to develop this theme a little bit more than what it is right now. There are a lot of possibilities. This is just the start. Today, people don't do enough research on a subject so they can change their minds about it. It can be proven statistically and historically what has happened in this country. There are people who have suffered from it. They are alive, but no thanks to Wall Street!

4

Jazmin, 19

Date: Monday, October 24, 2011
Location: Between Jackson & LaSalle Street, Chicago, IL
Event: Occupy Chicago
Occupation: Nanny
Written Response

Jazmin Mohn from Des Plaines, Illinois answered strongly in her handwritten response as to why she was a participant in the *Occupy Movement*:

For change to occur action must be taken! I am here today to ensure my future and the generations to come. Without courage all is already lost! I am not afraid because without risk, without bravery, our world would still be facing slavery, segregation and other social and economic injustices. We are all human beings and I demand today that I be able to accomplish the same as the 1%!

5

Vicki

Date: Monday, October 24, 2011
Location: Between Jackson & LaSalle Street, Chicago, IL
Event: Occupy Chicago
Occupation: Real Estate Broker
Transcribed Voice Recording

There's a collection of reasons for why I'm here. There's not one single reason. If I were to sum it up in one word it would be *unfairness*. This is supposed to be a country of fair play and freedom of speech. I've lived long enough to know that I've had to fight for civil rights. I've had to fight for women's equal rights and in the Vietnam War. It's time for the silent majority to speak out. Thirty years of trickled down economics has simply failed. Now, it's time for our voices to be heard. Because we are a free society, if we don't exercise it (freedom) through such things as freedom of speech and the vote, then we are no better then a country that has no democracy. And yet, we can, in good conscience send our sons and daughters to war for the rights of citizens in Iraq and Afghanistan and other foreign countries. We have cheered on Middle Eastern uprisings, but they aren't peaceful protesters. We (the U.S.) are peaceful protesters. If our government and our media can support them (Middle Eastern uprisings) than they should be supporting us as we peacefully demonstrate. We've had enough of injustice and unfairness. *Occupy Wall Street* was 21 days into their demonstrations, peaceful demonstrations when I first heard about it. It was like the media tried to withhold it from us. And I'm sorry, in a country that prides itself in having Freedom of Speech that was the turning point for me. It was so reminiscent of the 60's, being shot at by the National Guard...it brought all of that stuff back to my memory and I said: "It's time." I was going to come last week, but I must be a fair weather protester (laughs) because it was too cold and windy last week! We are the 99% and it's not that we don't love and support the 1%. But when Congress, the majority of which are Republicans claim it's the 1% who provide jobs...but they clearly don't because we have watched them in the last twelve years, starting with George W. Bush. We gave them all the tax breaks, where are the jobs? But, guess what? Corporate greed has taken over. It's all about the race to the bottom for cheap labor. And I'm sorry, I'm tired of it. I want to see the same media that back when Ronald Reagan had the Fairness Doctrine, we had over 500 corporations that owned the media. Now there are only five. So the consolidation makes me ask what happened to Anti-trust? That was there so no one had to worry about corporations getting too big to fail. And I'm sick and tired of hearing people say the government is too big! I'm sorry, government is dysfunctional right now, but the only thing that has the whip to keep checks and balances in place for corporations so we don't become a plutocracy is government. Right now, the government is primarily occupied by the Republicans, but owned by the corporations. I'm tired of it. The trickled down economics has failed.

6

Melissa, 21

Date: Monday, October 24, 2011
Location: Between Jackson & LaSalle Street, Chicago, IL
Event: Occupy Chicago
Occupation: Server, Waitress
Written Response

Melissa, a server from Naperville, Illinois responded to why she was a participant in the *Occupy Movement* in a short, but meaningful and powerful handwritten response:

People need to come together and let the thieving corporations know they aren't going to keep quiet about the middle class shrinking. They are crooks! We are angry! Fairness and equality needs to happen. We're going to march until they do something to help us. We're all on this earth together and the money hungry are going to tear us apart. I am apart of the 99%!

7

Rob Burns, the Man with a Plan

Date: Monday, October 24, 2011
Location: Between Jackson & LaSalle Street, Chicago, IL
Event: Occupy Chicago
Age: 45
Occupation: Economist, Politician
Transcribed Voice Recording

I called Rob Burns the "Man with a Plan" because he was literally the only one I spoke to on this day who actually had plan for solving the problems in America. He humbly represents the small percentage of demonstrators who have an action plan which, in my view are the most threatening demonstrators to the powers that be. These kinds of protesters aren't just holding up a sign here or there, making various complaints, but ones like Rob have actually developed a strategy on how things can be made right. He's focused on an issue, created a strategy to solve it and figured out the appropriate way to carry it out. Now, this is the smart way to protest and achieve results! All he needs is a group of people to stand with him. In my opinion, all protesters need to follow his example. For more on Rob's plan keep reading.

Rob Burns: "I share so many of the frustrations of so many of the protesters here with the way the government is being hijacked, taken over by Wall Street and the other financial interests. I would like to see us have a financial system that serves our interests rather than forcing us to just serve them constantly with their insatiable appetite for more and more money, which basically drives us into despair and poverty. I see what we're doing here, like the way I like to characterize it is that we are trying to end the undue privilege our government is granting to these interests, who don't see it as a privilege at all because they think they're entitled to have that privilege. They think they just should run our monopoly, finance systems and the core fundamental parts of our economy. So I would like to see that brought to an end. That's why I came out. I've been working on stuff like this for quite a while. I ran for Congress last year as a Green Party candidate. I've been very frustrated with the way our economy and our government have been running for quite some time. When this whole protest began I was very excited to find there were a lot of other people who felt the same way I did. We've been sort of hidden from each other by the media, which only seems to present the Wall Street view of things, and so as soon as *Occupy Chicago* started happening I knew I needed to be apart of it."

The following information was retrieved from a flyer given to me from Rob. I have summarized the points of the plan. Please visit the website below for complete information.

Title: Path to Prosperity for US ALL (P2P4USA) Visit: http://path2prosperity4all.us/ for more details.

Purpose: The P2P4USA Plan is dedicated to placing the United States on a solid political economic foundation for a prosperous and democratic future.

There should be a constitutional amendment to:

1. Enact a one time only progressive net worth tax to reverse the widening distribution of wealth, income and political power undermining our democracy...
2. Repay all personal debt for everyone in the U.S. to reset our economy and eliminate the structural debt that otherwise will never be repaid...
3. Repay all privately held federal debt and require a balanced federal budget...
4. Buy back at full value all fictitious asset paper claims designed to redistribute wealth from those who work to those who do not work...
5. Restore to a comparable home all those foreclosed upon and evicted since 2008, due to the systematic failures from the financial housing crisis...
6. End corporate personhood and end ignoble privilege...

7. Require all revenues for natural resources and natural monopoly resources accrue only to public treasuries...

8. Require governments to ensure that no involuntary servitude arises whenever we must sell ourselves on the job market...

9. Establish a federalist delegation of stewardship over natural resources...

The initiative further duly prioritizes the needs of retirees and the disabled over the whims of Wall Street. It establishes Medicare...with universal health coverage and provides abundant funding of higher education to promote an educated population without soul-crushing student loans...

What can you do?

1. Visit the website above to learn more. Understand the issues and the possibilities and profound potential for reform.

2. Consider involving yourself in a third-party or independent run for office (either your own campaign or someone else's) especially for state legislator, U.S. House, or U.S. Senate and make P2P4USA a part of the campaign platform.

8

Taylor Stekkinger

Date: Monday, October 24, 2011
Location: Between Jackson & LaSalle Street, Chicago, IL
Event: Occupy Chicago
Age: 18
Occupation: "Chicago"
Transcribed Voice Recording

I'm Taylor Stekkinger. I'm 18 years old and unemployed. What happened was in my high school in the city where I used to live they didn't like "bad kids." They do whatever they can to weed them out of their schools. And so they said I wasn't paying attention or whatever and they wanted to send me to a psychiatrist so they could prescribe me with drugs, but me and my mom refused it. So after that the school decided they were going to kick me out. I got into a couple of fights and things like that. Then they threw me out and put me into an alternative school, which was completely terrible. They locked us in everyday. They had guards in every hallway. There were at least three fights everyday. So I dropped out because it was just like, it was ridiculous. The whole experience shows how the system doesn't treat kids properly. If kids are having a hard time learning you're not supposed to weed them out, you're not supposed to give them drugs and things like that. Before I dropped out of high school though, we actually got our house foreclosed on, so we moved to California and that's when I dropped out of school. After asking my self why is all of this going on? Why are they trying to give me drugs, why did I get kicked out of my high school? I mean, I know it's my own actions of course but I think it's a little drastic to kick someone out. Why did my house get foreclosed on? Why is all of this happening at the same time? And why does it seem like everybody is suffering from the same problems? When I dropped out of high school I did a lot of research on my own which sparked my interest in the Wall Street Movement when it started and then when I heard about the *Occupy Chicago* I just headed on over here and joined in. I'm here because of my background. All these problems are happening. I feel rejected by the education system. We've been thrown out of our house. We've had a hard time affording food, things like that. I've filled out at least a hundred applications and I still can't get a job. I know I don't have an education, but still why can't I at least get a job at a fast food restaurant or a coffee shop? I've literally filled out hundreds of applications and still...nothing. That's pretty much why I'm here because I've had a lot of issues in my life, even psychologically. I was diagnosed with ADHD which I believe is a direct cause from watching television. Television is designed to make us think a certain way. Like *Jersey Shore*. *Jersey Shore* is about a lot of drama, but life really isn't like that. It's psychological warfare through T.V. You watch a channel and then what? A commercial followed by another commercial followed by another commercial. Then it's back to the show and then commercial, commercial, commercial! It makes your brain crazy, jumping from one thing to another. There are other things too. Like, why is good food more expensive than bad food? Why is our water filled with lead and other contaminants? Why is everything being capitalized on? Dropping out of high school was a really big thing for me, but after that I started self-educating myself and learning the truth. I stopped watching mainstream media which is full of lies and advertisements. I started looking for better news sources. One of my personal favorites is an online news website, *RT.com*. I also like to read books. I'm just kind of educating myself about what is going on here. To me, I see nothing but people being enslaved. Here in Chicago, I see cameras on every street corner. I see police totally disregarding "to serve and protect." They've been harassing us. Like, for example when protesters were arrested on Saturday (October 22, 2011) I was at the jail Sunday afternoon, waiting for them to be released. I went there around noon and I asked the police why the protesters were being held. I started asking legal questions, but they refused to give me an answer. They were very rude. They told me to shut up. They screamed at me. They said that if I stayed and asked questions I would be arrested too, things like that. The police aren't doing their job. Like, I understand wanting to keep people safe, but doing things like this isn't keeping people safe because what they're doing is wrong. They've made city ordinance laws, such as not being able to stay in a public park after 11:00 p.m. I think that's absolutely absurd...it's a public park! Another law is that we can't have any of our personal belongings on the sidewalk. Nothing can be stationary. We have to keep moving with our things. We can't stand still on the sidewalk without the cops harassing us about it. Another thing, why is there no free parking? There are plenty of streets in Chicago where people can park. There are parking signs for absolutely no reason. It doesn't help traffic. It doesn't make sense. This government capitalizes off of everything it can. They're here to only make money. That's why I'm here. I see all these things going on in my life and I see everybody suffering much worse here and overseas. I mean, we've (the U.S.) infiltrated countries we should've never gone into. You know, Iraq was never any of our business. Libya isn't any of our business. And now, Africa isn't any of our business either. We've been wasting our money. Fifty-eight percent of our budget is spent on military purposes. You know how much is spent on healthcare? Like ten or twenty percent! How can you (the government) spend that little money on health and 58% on death? That's why I'm here because I see it all going on. I've experienced it and it's very apparent. To people who are for the movement but aren't out here with us I say we need you here. I understand people have their jobs and they have to go to work, but everybody needs to start coming whenever they get a chance. The more bodies we have, the more awareness we raise and it just helps the movement overall. Numbers are our biggest thing. When people see a lot of people hanging out they start asking questions, which is what we want people to do. To those who are against the movement, those who drive by and yell at us, saying things like: "Get a job, you dumb hippies!" To those who completely reject us all I can say is...without being negative because in reality it's not their fault. It's the fault of the mass media. They've manipulated these people to be on their side. And it's really not their fault. They really just don't understand yet. But there will be a time when the numbers will grow. *Occupy Wall Street* is getting bigger. *Occupy Chicago* is growing and there are thousands of movements similar to what we're doing right here going on all over. There are revolutions taking place in Europe, the one in Libya and soon people will start caring about this at least enough to start asking questions. Hopefully they'll start thinking clearly something must be wrong here if all these people are here. And when the time comes they'll go on strike and support the movement. I've been with *Occupy Chicago* since day three. Since I've been here I've learned that basically the broad idea of the movement is to end corporate control and a greed driven system. Some would argue that, that is purely capitalism. Some would say that reason isn't good enough. Either way, we need to fight to end corporate greed. We need to fight to end the Federal Reserve. It really upsets me when the media claims we (protesters) don't know what we're protesting for. That's not true. Some of us just don't have a set of demands yet because we're trying to organize with the masses. That's the point of this, raising awareness...so ending corporate greed is, in my view, the main idea of the movement. Now, when I arrived here on day three there were about fourteen people lined up against the Federal Reserve Building right here between Jackson & LaSalle. We had a small amount of supplies. We had a couple tents and we had some tarps. Now on this day the police came up to us and told us we were not allowed to pitch tents and that it was against a city ordinance. So, that was the number one thing from cops. So we slept under the tarps and it was terrible. It was a terrible night. It rained really hard over us. We put a tarp up with some poles and tape and kind of made a whole tarp system, but then it completely collapsed on us in the middle of the night! All of our bedding was completely soaked. It was wet and it was raining. It was freezing! It was so cold. But, I mean, I think it was that night that made all of this so great because it showed how dedicated we were to the movement in general. And those original fourteen people are still here. They are still here. Some of them are here 24/7, some leave and come back. But every person I met that day is still here. On day four, we did some general assemblies and marched. When we came back from the march the cops were there to tell us we were not allowed to camp near the Federal Reserve Building period. They said anywhere near the pillars, located in the front of the building was federal property and we needed to leave immediately. So we packed up our things and moved to another location. Once we settled there the cops told us we couldn't stay in that location either. The rules kept changing. The police kept playing games with us. Like, I guess they were thinking: "Well, let's push them back little by little until this whole thing ends," but they completely failed...

Unfortunately, due to mechanical problems at least 30 minutes of Taylor's testimony was cut from the interview. However, I do remember:

- Taylor mentioning the fact that the G8 Summit would be held in Chicago, Illinois in May of 2012. He mentioned the mounting excitement of being able to protest there. He said he hopes it will be a peaceful demonstration, but expressed concern that it may not be.
- Despite Taylor's obvious grief with law enforcement, I do want to point out that during the interview he mentioned how he and other protesters had actually spoken with many policemen during demonstrations, reminding them that they are simply pawns in a game of chess. Taylor says that many police men and women have agreed with the protesters and even apologized while arresting them.
- Taylor mentioning the importance of referring to each other as brother and sister regardless of background. He said it united the protesters and gave them unity.

Taylor Stekkinger is a strong, young man, full of energy and he and others like him are exactly what this protest needs.

9

Chicago Police

In the previous chapter, Taylor Stekkinger mentioned the fact that he and the rest of the protesters often spoke peacefully to police officers during demonstrations, reminding them that they were simply pawns being used in a game of chess. He also said that many police officers apologized while arresting some protesters because, perhaps inwardly they agreed with the demonstrations. I tried to speak with a Chicago police officer myself on the evening of October 24th, but he declined the interview. However, he stated to me that he was not in opposition to the movement at all. After holding this brief conversation with him I couldn't help but wonder where all the understanding of the movement could possibly lead to.

Is this the beginning of an *Occupy Police* and other *Occupy* you-fill-in-the-blanks? Just think about it, law enforcement, along with the military are the only ones who are responsible for maintaining social order. In the author's opinion, they follow all the orders and carry out all the duties prescribed by the 1%. If they should decide at any moment to collectively abandon their responsibilities wouldn't the entire United States government be forced to reckon with the 99%? My question is why are the police taking up for the 1%, a group that hardly recognizes them at all; a group that doesn't even consider them to be apart of an elite system that seems to only treat them nice when they really need them; especially during times like this.

10

Radio, 18

Date: Monday, October 24, 2011
Location: Between Jackson & LaSalle Street, Chicago, IL
Event: Occupy Chicago
Age: 18
Occupation: Activist, Educator
Written Response

Radio was sure to place a note on her written response to my question which read: *Note: Please do not rephrase or change the vocabulary.* Very well, Radio. Your wish is my command.

When Radio was asked why she was a participant in the *Occupy Chicago* movement she wrote:

Hey! As an independent woman who has lived in Chicago for the majority of my life I find it imperative to represent my demographic. All demographics should be required to represent themselves; for they too are the 99%! On a personal level, however, I am here to represent my people. I am a band member of the *Bad River Ojibwe*. But I am also here to bring awareness to the lies and hypocrisy within the current democratic system of the United States.

I find that humans who claim to represent "the people" need to do their job! Represent the 100%, not just the fat cats. We need to stabilize our country and our world. Put the power back in the hands of the people and not in the mattresses of the 1%! I hope that in the end we achieve our goals. I hope that this is all worth it. To those reading, take this to heart; for this quote has been passed around as a common phrase for encouragement: "First they ignore you. Then they laugh at you. Then they fight you. Then you win." -Ghandi

11

Dante Alexander, 20

Date: Monday, October 24, 2011
Location: Between Jackson & LaSalle Street, Chicago, IL
Event: Occupy Chicago
Age: 20
Occupation: Student
Transcribed Voice Recording

Dante: I want to start by saying I'm here because I feel that if you don't stand for anything you'll fall for anything. Basically, I feel like the governments are too corrupt. It's time for all this to end. Not just the government, but the banks and all the other people up there. It's time for everything to stop and for the world, for us to actually have our rights, the rights that we were given...our constitutional rights. The laws that we're supposed to have every day that law officials break and kick dirt upon. So that's why I'm here.

Hannah Faye: What do you say to people who disagree with you; people who disagree and just want to go on living their regular lives.

Dante: I say to them, what is a regular life? Because it's definitely not this. This is not freedom. We don't have freedom of speech.

Hannah Faye: How do you want to conclude?

Dante: This (protesting) is what democracy looks like. This is what I'm here for. This is what I'll stay here for until things change.

Hannah Faye: Are you prepared to stay until whenever?

Dante: Yeah, I am, 'til next year, next week, ten years from now...'til whenever.

Hannah Faye: You have no intentions at all whatsoever of leaving?

Dante: No, I don't.

Hannah Faye: What do you say to people who aren't here?

Dante: If they want to sit around and watch the revolution that's fine by me, but I'm going to be apart of it. I'm going to be remembered for what I'm doing here.

Hannah Faye: What was the turning point for you where you realized this was not something you were just going to watch on T.V., but something you were going to be apart of?

Dante: That was actually last Wednesday when we decided on the action that took place on Saturday (October 22, 2011). Last Saturday, our goal was to occupy property near Congress and Michigan. I wouldn't say it was a fail, but we exceeded the point we were at before that time. And no, we didn't take what we wanted but what we did that day still meant something to all of us. I, myself got arrested along with 150 other people. But that comes with pride. It just came with so much pride and passion. I knew that, not on that day, but when we first brought up the idea to take action, I knew I needed to be apart of that. This is why I'm here and this is why I'll stay here.

12

Charles Reese, 43

Date: Monday, October 24, 2011
Location: Between Jackson & LaSalle Street, Chicago, IL
Event: Occupy Chicago
Occupation: Business Owner
Transcribed Voice Recording

The reason why I'm here is because I want a better future for us all, especially for the young people. I want better healthcare for our people. I'm here to fight for what our economy needs to be. It needs to get better. That's why I'm here. I'm also here because we all need to just learn how to get along with one another. I've always had a heart for the people. I've always felt that we've been too far apart. The love that we're supposed to have for one another isn't there. We've been too segregated. People have been too segregated throughout my life. I'm 43 years old, so I think it's about time for us all to come together and I think it's good that we're all together right here right now at this point in time. It's sad to say that things had to happen like this in order for us to come together, but it's a big step towards something positive and I'm just keeping the faith that the things I mentioned will come to pass. This is a time when we all need to come together and make things happen concerning the things we've been complaining about; the things we've had problems with throughout the majority of our lives. This is the time now to voice your opinion, your feelings and to speak out for the things you've been concerned about all this time. I mean, before you become apart of something you should pray about it first. You shouldn't do anything without praying first. So pray about it and allow the Lord to be your director in the things you should say and do. But, this is the time for people to get up and let their voices be heard. Wake up people! Don't be deceived, continuously throughout your life. It's nothing but the Enemy who's confusing you. Just, wake up. I love

35

all my brothers and sisters that are here, whether they are white, black, whatever color they are, whatever race that they're in, it doesn't matter. I love you all. Keep your heads up. Keep God first and continue to pray. Like the word of God says: "We'll all rise..." His people will rise and we are all rising.

13

Steve, 55

Date: Monday, October 24, 2011
Location: Between Jackson & LaSalle Street, Chicago, IL
Event: Occupy Chicago
Transcribed Voice Recording

The interview with a man named Stephen Steele would be my last one for the day; for it was now evening and anyone will tell you Chicago's evening cool is a bitter one. I was cold, hungry and ready to go home. But I wanted one more interview. However, most of the protesters had gone home and the streets which overflowed earlier with occupancy were now bare with just a few faithful demonstrators. Amongst those was Stephen. For short, he asked me to call him Steve. Steve is homeless. During the interview, he told me he'd just been released from a nursing home. I didn't ask why. He said he'd been sick and not feeling well, but that he would be delighted to express his opinions for my book. He said and I quote: "I think I have something to say."

Steve: "Number one, I'm here because I'm homeless. I had a job, I got sick, I was in a nursing home...I'm just out here because somebody has to make a change. Protests like this went on in the 60's, with the civil rights movement. I'd like to see it like that again, but it's so convoluted. I'm going to tell you the truth. It's a lot of problems. It's a lot of problems going on right here. People don't know what they want to do. A couple days ago, ten minutes to eleven I knew when it came to that park they (the police) were going to arrest everybody. If you're on the Eastside of Michigan Avenue you're going to get arrested. So I left. Why occupy the jails? Why put more money into the police department? They (the police) were giggling, standing up there, putting on their gloves and saying things like: "We're making over time." If we can just get one mind...my church is always talking about one mind. If it's about God, if it's about whatever you are doing...if everybody has one mind something can be done. You know, last night they (the protesters) were arguing at 11 o'clock whether or not they want to go over here to the Thompson Center or stay at the park. You know what's going to happen on Congress and Michigan (the park). You want to be arrested twice? It doesn't make sense to me, I don't know. Like I said, I'm homeless right now. I'm here because I'm hoping that maybe this will bring about a change. It's a lot of good people around here and we're looking after each other. We have a place to sleep at night. We have food, clothing, etc. It's like this...it (the protests) just came up and I like to help out. I don't like to make a lot of noise. I'm an older dude, you know? All these kids, these are kids around here, seventeen, eighteen years old, they don't seem to mind going to jail. But I can't go to jail. Some of them, they leave from here and then they go back to the suburbs. They come here, maybe spend about three or four days and then they want to go home. And they (unknown persons) pay for them to go home. That freaks me out. I just found that out yesterday. They're paying for people to go to Minnesota and other places. Everybody doesn't have the option to leave the protests. In fact, nobody has an option. If you think about it mostly everybody is one or two paychecks away from being on the streets, you know? That's no joke. I've been having some medical problems and I just came out of the nursing home and so I'm out here. At least somebody is trying to make a change. Somebody is trying to do something for us (the homeless). Where would I have gotten this chili from tonight? God is good. God is good. I don't know where I would be right now if I wasn't here. But me, I'm not a loud guy. I hate to say it but if you ask fifty people down here what the agenda is, you're going to get fifty different answers. I'm sorry to say. They're getting close to having a core agenda. We're getting close, but you know everybody has different problems. This is not just going to go away. For the people who are lackadaisical about all of this, the ones who just don't care...their time is going to come. They're going to find out what's happening and what's not going to be happening for them. Like I said, when the paychecks stop, when the social security stops...they can't depend on anything. Look, the government took my link card away from me. They're constantly laying people off all over. Everybody has to pay attention. I sell newspapers in the morning. But people don't read newspapers now. My job is about to be folded.

Everybody's got I-pads and I-pods, lap-tops, and blackberries. They're on the internet, at work reading a paper.

Hannah Faye: What do you say to people who refuse to participate in anything like this?

Steve: I don't say. I don't have any words for them. We had people barking at us coming out from the Board of Trade right over there (points across the street). What are you going to do about that? A guy came by, not too long ago in a Lamborghini and mocked us. This is a non-violent protest. That's the way I'd like to keep it in my heart. I'm not going to get into any mess with anybody else.

Hannah Faye: Do you have any last words?

Steve: Go with God. If everybody had one mind it's going to get done. Go with God and be of one mind. That's it.

Occupy Wall Street 2011

To the Reader

Unlike the day I chose to interview the Chicagoan protesters, October 29, 2011 was a very bad day to interview the New Yorkers. Temperatures dropped to the mid 30's, the winds were at 24 mph and what started out as rain turned into snow! It was blistering cold and foggy. To add to my frustration, many of the train lines were shut down and I had to find alternate routes walking blocks and blocks in my wet Converse. If I'd known the weather was going to be like that I would've at least brought three pairs of gloves and boots. It was so cold at some points I could literally not feel my hands or feet. And I could only think: if it's like this now what will it be like for protesters come mid-December?

That morning though, even before I left the guesthouse to meet with the protesters I thought to myself. I thought maybe I shouldn't go to Occupy Wall Street. Forget it, I wasn't going to go. I looked outside at the weather and thought maybe I should just wait until tomorrow. But then a thought came to me. If I went out today in the very far-from-being perfect weather wouldn't I get the testimonies of the rain-or-shine protesters? The protesters who didn't care what the weather was like. If I interviewed them under these conditions wouldn't that speak volumes of the protesters themselves? Wouldn't it speak of their determination? What would be the significance of interviewing them on a day like this? And so, I grabbed my notebook, my recorder and headed for Wall Street.

When I finally arrived on Wall Street, at the camp of the protesters I could not believe my eyes. Unlike Chicagoans, the New Yorkers had pushed for rights to pitch tents. There were so many of them spread throughout Liberty Park (Zucotti Park) it reminded me of a campsite. To my surprise, they were also allowed to spend the night in these tents. Further inquiry led to my understanding that in this same place a medical center, a comfort center, and even a kitchen had been established. The New York protesters are highly advanced. They have organized themselves and the details of running a literally free society.

14

Dawn, 49

Date: Saturday, October 29, 2011
Location: Wall Street, New York
Event: Occupy Wall Street
Occupation: Photographer
Transcribed Voice Recording

I am a participant at Wall Street. I'm from Brooklyn. I'm here protesting because it's come to a point in my life where I'm left with no choice. I'm out here protesting to the government about how I'm living and what I'm going through. I'm protesting here. It was hard for me...all my life was a struggle. I never had a career on Wall Street because I was mostly out there. I got government funds to help me, but they weren't much. Today I'm here...I'm older now. The world has changed. This is where I thought I would finally find peace and serenity, amongst protesters. All my life I didn't know where to go to find help. I've been through the system. It never helped me at all. It was a complete joke. I've gone to government offices and practically begged for help. The population in the world today is phenomenal. People are coming from all over the world just to come to New York. It seems like we're running out of words, we're running out of speech, we're running out of politicians and we're all at each other's throats. It's become a joke and a hate game. The hatred has built up so highly that it brings tears to people's eyes. You can walk down the street; especially here in Manhattan on Wall Street which I feel is such a shame. The executives, stock brokers...you can tell on their faces they ignore it, they don't know what to do about it anymore. We're all grabbing on to that hope. We're saying please help us. What do we do from here? Then God says the world's coming to an end. I don't know what to do anymore because I'm in a holding place. When people turn on each other God sees it. But sometimes I wonder: Where is he (God)? Where is he? You (God) won't hold me. Then I have to carry this with me. I get a small income from the government for my disability. I can protest all day long but they're not going to give me any more. I can go into my social security office today and I won't get any more help. I've asked for it several times. They say I'm lucky I got that check and send me on my way. I've tried to make it in the world but I just can't. I've had several places to live, but I just can't afford it. My budget doesn't include taking care of my health. They say: here, take this. This is all the wealth we can give you. They say: here's a roof over your head, but how can I live unhealthy once I'm inside? It doesn't work. I've tried it. I mean, I've been talked about in apartment complexes. I've been ashamed. People look at me and wonder when I'm going to change my clothes. They're thinking: when is she going to have something nice for herself. It's just really disrespectful. So I say I'm happy to be here with the protesters for that reason. I have to stand out in the cold, under a tree and cry and ask God if he can please help fight with me for change...I ask him: can you help us make a change? You know, people might look at us like we're a bunch of freaks, but we're not. We would all love to move into some beautiful place and wear nice clothes but there's a lot of hatred here. There are too many people. I would like to go back to the country myself. I'm from the country, but Rheumatism has got me stopped when it comes to traveling. It makes it hard to live. It takes your self-esteem away. A lot of self-esteem is lost even by being a protester. But we need to stop this poorness in the country. Politicians don't even come by and at least ask us what we want. They don't ask us why we're out here. They just hear rumors: they're just protesting and everyone has a different goal. There are. Some protesters are fighting for their jobs. Some of them are fighting for their family life. Some are fighting because they're homeless. A lot of them are ashamed to admit they're homeless. I don't think that's right. They need to be honest and say they're homeless. They're protesting because they have a right to live in some place. We're people. The law has allowed us to be together, to pull together through this. It's rough. Each one of us has had a bad life. What we should be fighting for is the idea to come to politician's minds: that they've (homeless) been out there long enough. We (politicians) can build a nice, big monument for them to live in and they can achieve their working status from there and stop relying on government funds.

But by prolonging this, knowing we're out here and not at least coming by, getting involved and cleaning this mess up they're just showing they don't care and they really don't support us. By sitting behind the desk, throwing threats around is not the right thing to do because it could cause violence. It could cause hysteria. There's a lot of stereotyping going on right now. It's not healthy. Business men and women can't get their jobs done properly with pain and suffering going on. How do you work from 9 to 5 knowing you have to walk through this (Occupy Wall Street) everyday? And you have to go home and worry about how your life is going to end up. By assaulting these people (protesters)...if the cops say: we'll put our foot down and take these people out of there. It's not going to help. They go into the streets and push around people just because they feel like it's going to help; but it's not going to help. It doesn't cure the problem going after the people. You can't judge us by the way we look. You don't know the other side to me. I could put on a dress like I'm going to work and be the healthiest woman in the world, but not living in a tent. I do get a check from the government because I have a bad injury which crippled me. But tears come to my eyes every day because I wonder if they'll (the government) put their foot down one day and take from us (the disabled). I don't want anybody to take from me. What do I have? I need the money. I need to save money to get out of the mess I'm in. Then the thought comes to me: I need to go get a job, but it's tough. You can't go to a job when you have to clean your body with baby wipes. It is embarrassing to live this way. So I don't know what result will come out of this but as long as I'm here I'm going to fight for the property rights. It is a park (Liberty Park), but we can change it into a nice apartment complex or a condo. From here, I don't know what's going to take place. All I know is that I've protested my life and I'm going to keep protesting no matter if it's here or if it's out of town. I've got to go with my people. I can't wonder around the streets anymore. I can't. I cry for my children. I have children. I can't be in their lives because of the position I'm in. Thank God, they made it out there. I don't know how, but they made it. My son is married with a wife and two children. I'm here just for me right now. I'm going to stick with the protesters. I just live one day at a time. I live and let live. I'm a liberal. I'm a woman of the world. When I found this place (Occupy Wall Street) I didn't know anything about it, but when I did find it I was really happy. I found a part of me that was buried. I thank God today that I'm here because it let so much out of me. It freed danger from my life. Because I'm here I have more hope than what I had before. When I protest I keep it in my mind that I'm the 99% and that's important for people to know. That's about it. Thank you.

15

Rhachi, 22

Date: Saturday, October 29, 2011
Location: Wall Street, New York
Event: Occupy Wall Street
Occupation: Struggling Lyricist
Transcribed Voice Recording

I want to speak clearly. I feel like we're (protesters) making history and I want to be apart of that. I'm so thankful to God that I could be apart of history and history in the making. It's a work in progress. It's progressively progressing. It's beautiful! I think it's such a beautiful thing. Honestly, I think it's God's will. I started being apart of this just walking by it everyday, right? Because I had recently broke up with my girlfriend and she kicked me out. I've known her since I was eight years old. I'm in love with her. Anyway, I'm 22 years old and I'm just tired. You know what I mean? I'm tired. I'm tired of chasing. I figured if I started hanging out in Manhattan I would probably get a lot further in life rather than hanging out on Staten Island. I've been living on Staten Island for 22 years. I always had God in my life and always wanted to be a good person but people don't make it very easy to be a good person, you know what I mean? I used to say this to God: God, if you don't give me what I want and what I want out of life, I'm not working for you no more. Like, if you could put God in front of me, I would say that to him. And I've said it to him. I know God is real. I know God is very real. I don't care what anyone says. I know God is real. You understand what I mean? I'm fighting to be apart of this (Occupy Wall Street). And I don't care if I die doing it. I just want to be involved. I'll go out like Tupac. I'm not fighting for anything specific. I'm fighting for their (the protesters) cause. Whatever they're fighting for...the 99%...we are the 99% and that 1%, those people who are money hungry...the scum bags, counting money while they see us sleeping in the park, in the rain, and then they drive by in their limos, Lexuses, or whatever the fuck they got and they go...I mean, some of them are good people. I've met some really rich guys that are nice because they're good people and they have faith in God. I've gotten financial advice from them and they've said to me if I just have faith in God everything will happen for me. And I believe that. I believe I have a promising future. What I'm saying is, even if this (the recording) doesn't go out...even if you (Hannah Faye) lose this tape and my words never go out I still have a future. You're going to still remember what I said. I can only be true. I can't do certain things anymore. I told God: all I want is you, nothing else. I remember one day I was either going to hurt myself or I was going to hurt somebody else, but it didn't happen. I'm just glad to be alive today doing this (the recording) here with you. I want the world to change. I don't want it to be a monarchy or a democracy or a republic. See what they (U.S.) say is: in God we trust and they use God to scare people. America uses God to scare people. I know that. The people (law makers) who sat down in that room a long time ago in Georgia or Maryland or wherever the fuck it was...they didn't know what they were doing really. They just tried. I mean, they probably were good people, but I don't think the people who have that power now are using that power in the right way. I don't think they're (law makers) still doing it for God, like presidents, Bush and other people. I think Barack Obama is a really God fearing person though. I think he lives for the struggle. He's Jewish. And the fundamental of Judaism is "each one, teach one how to serve each other and how to serve God and how to teach each other how to have a relationship with God." In Hebrew it sounds very beautiful, but I forgot how to say it in Hebrew. That's what we need...a relationship with God. God is real. I can't say anything negative to people who are against this (Occupy Wall Street). Dude, I don't even know if they're going to read this. I don't know...just pay it forward. I don't believe there are bad people in this world. There's no such thing as a bad person, but I do believe there are some wicked people. You see them (wicked people) via 9/11 or by other terrorist acts. But to people who are against this: if you see someone that honestly looks like they need something help them out, have faith in God and just be the best person you can be. Chivalry is not dead. I've seen it very vividly. God is real.

Good people do exist. I believe everybody tries. People are just caught up in their own way of thinking and beliefs. Everyone has a way of twisting their way of thinking into their own beliefs and twisting their beliefs into their own way of thinking. I never said that like that before. I like the way I said that (laughs).

Hannah Faye: So you said you are a struggling lyricist?

Rhachi: Yeah. You want me to do something right now?

Hannah Faye: Can you?

Rhachi: Yeah.

Hannah Faye: Can you say something about this event (Occupy Wall Street)?

Rhachi: Yeah.

Hannah Faye: You sure?

Rhachi: Yeah. I wrote something about this.

Hannah Faye: Okay. I want you to put your final words in it.

Rhachi: (NOTE to Rhachi from Hannah Faye: I'm sorry if I totally hammered this. Transcribing this was hard as hell.) Trust me on this. Yo, I walk around like my dick is enormous, knowing damn well my shit is the smallest, but bitches be on it. I'm sorry. These pigeons and chickens be squawkin' but they never leave my crib disappointed. It's a whole different story. You see I'ma stick to the point when I say I'm beyond what these lil niggas is talkin. I'm really crazy...7:30, like that shit in the mornin' like fresh make up, motherfucker. Early, wake up, motherfucker. With fresh eggs and bacon, motherfucker. Yeah, it's hot! Fix a plate up motherfucker and don't you waste it motherfucker 'cause some little kids in Africa would be grateful, motherfucker. You understand? Yo, in God's eyes I've been trying to move from failure to favor but I've been losing for so long I feel like I'm failing by nature. I could go to jail for a case or either these drug sales or whatever the

48

fuck, whatever truck sales for the paper. I just spazzed, control starts to fail cause my anger and yet I wake up every day and I still give people a challenge. I'm still pure in every way but I gotta live with imbalance. For what it's worth while I'm on earth I leave these kids with some knowledge. So when I'm gone, God willing I'm still in thoughts like I was Christopher Wallace. If inspiration was a liq I'd have the shit by the gallons. But it's so easily said that's why I'm living in silence. This shit is a challenge, most niggas is smilin. They just children though. I'm messin' with the essence. I express the way I pray and flow. I'm very passionate about my shit. As you can see, as you (Hannah Faye) take a tape and you gonna smash all about my shit, just smash it together and cram it together however you can, but I'm just so glad that she (Hannah Faye) sat there with a pen and she actually took the time, five minutes maybe we took it to ten...(laughs)

16

Lilibeth Castanedo, 22

Date: Saturday, October 29, 2011
Location: Wall Street, New York
Event: Occupy Wall Street
Occupation: Activist
Transcribed Voice Recording

When asked how long she'd been a participant in the Occupy Wall Street movement, Lilibeth answered:

"What constitutes being here, really? Living here? Camping here? Or being apart of the movement and being active within it?"

When asked what her occupation was she answered:

"What do you mean by occupation? I'm a revolutionary. I work in an Activist Collective (Epifaneo), but it's not for monetary value. It's for self-worth. It's for knowledge. It's to be in an environment with people I can learn from and people who can learn from me. Together, we develop organically from one another. We try to create an atmosphere where people can come and feel comfortable on stage, talk about what they advocate and put the word out there."

When asked why she was participating in the movement she answered:

"I'm here because we're (the people) in desperate need of awakening. We need unity amongst everybody. If it's going to take us being uncomfortable, becoming cold and pitching tents in a fucking park in the middle of New York City to bring awareness, to bring enlightenment, to cause a ripple in society for people to understand, for people to be interested and to inquire, to be intrigued, we're going to do it. We're going to stay here for as long as it takes for there to be some change from what we've built. We're an example of the kind of community we want to see in the world. We've been here since September (2011). Since then we've created this entire community. There's a kitchen, a medical station, a comfort station...anything you need you can find here. Everyone is welcoming and there is no monetary exchange. I've always felt I had to rise against things that were wrong. I've always felt like I had to speak my mind about things I felt strongly about. Whether it was little, insignificant things like wearing uniforms in school to major things. It's just a matter of standing up for what you believe in and being resilient. It's worth it. This is our life. We shouldn't settle for mediocrity just because it gives us financial security. We should be sacrificing our financial security to acquire the value of life so we can acquire happiness, love, everything that seems impossible and magical and unrealistic. I feel that instead of judging us as socialist or anti-capitalists, people should be receptive to what we have to say as we (the people) are receptive to everything they have to say. We would welcome them if they were to come into our community and speak their mind. This isn't just a community of likeminded individuals. Everyone here has their own fucking things to advocate. Everybody here has their own organization that they represent and we're always challenging one another, getting involved in heavy arguments. But, in the end we come to a consensus. That's what it's all about...being knowledgeable, spreading the knowledge and then coming to a consensus. That's an important thing. And the people who don't agree with us, the ones who don't even take the time to come down here and talk with us, those people can't change anything."

When asked for final words Lilibeth replied:

"It's difficult to think of...words that sum up everything I feel and believe for what I'm fighting for when I'm freezing cold...with my fingers numb, rolling cigarettes for the cause, just because. But I'll leave you with a song quote. What I feel is quite beautiful and quite relevant. It is: 'The people of the sun return to free the righteous children." And that's a beautiful line. And I feel like that's good enough to put on my poster board. So you can do what you will with that. What are your thoughts, if I may ask?

Hannah Faye: I'm with it 100%. I wish there were more teachers out here...

Lilibeth: Well, we're all teachers (in a sense).

Hannah Faye: Well, right. But there's a lot wrong with the education system in America today. Kids don't need to know trigonometry more than they need to know how to treat one another.

Lilibeth: You know what it is when it comes to the educational system? I'll give you an example that I learned a little while ago that I thought was kind of funny. The difference is that in America, teachers show kids the image of a cat along with the name, C-A-T. In any other country teachers will show you the picture of the cat, where the cat evolved from, all the different kinds of cats that there are, what diseases cats may spread, etc. They tell you everything there is to know about cats so that you have knowledge about them. Here, we simply connect the picture to the name and that's all there is to it. Basically, this is all you have to know and that's not knowledge. Kids leave high school these days not knowing shit. Why aren't the worst schools the most funded? Why aren't the best teachers in the worst schools teaching the kids who need them the most? That makes no sense. This is what needs to change.

Hannah Faye: Anything else Lili?

Lilibeth: It's fucking cold, man (laughs).

17

Jimmy Chen

Date: Saturday, October 29, 2011
Location: Wall Street, New York
Event: Occupy Wall Street
Transcribed Voice Recording

I am a participant in the Occupy Wall Street movement. The reason why I'm here is because it seems like the whole world is with the CCP, the Chinese Communist Party. It's about time for us to wake up and say no to the CCP! They murdered innocent Chinese people! They murdered over a hundred million Chinese people. It's about time for us to wake up, say something and do something. China made many people in the U.S. jobless. I watched the Occupy Wall Street on the news. I saw the kids on the news and they are trying to change the society into the right thing. I support them and I give them a lot of credit. People need to wake up and tell their congress it's time for them to act against the Communist Party in China. They also need to do the right thing for the people behind me (the protesters). Those kids (the protesters) deserve a better life. God bless America.

18

"Jennifer"

Date: Saturday, October 29, 2011
Location: Wall Street, New York
Event: Occupy Wall Street
Age: 30
Transcribed Voice Recording

The reason I'm a participant in the Occupy Wall Street movement is because one, I'm unemployed. Two, there are a limited amount of jobs now. There are actually none. I would like for things to change for people that have worked or people that are trying to go to school or people that are even in the shelter system, such as my self. They (unidentified persons) are sending people from the shelter system to Occupy Wall Street. So, that let's you know a lot about what's going on. It makes me angry, frustrated. I'm tired of going through this. I'm tired of going through the unemployment and the fact that the government is lying about being in debt. They claim they don't know how to fix things, but I believe they do. They just don't want to. My turning point was when...I'm homeless living on the streets first of all. I've been sleeping in Penn Station. Now they've been arresting people for sleeping in their station. I was sleeping in the subway station on the subway. I didn't feel like I was getting anything accomplished. I wasn't really doing anything. I felt that I was alone. What happened was someone suggested that I participate in Occupy Wall Street and I just decided one day. All the homeless people decided they were just going to come down. So I decided to and I went. I came here because again, first of all the shelter was sending people here. If I was to go back to the shelter they would send me here. And then again, I came for the cause. I came to support...I came for support. I'm trying to get the message out to the government and other people who are higher up.

Hannah Faye: What would have to happen in order for you to leave Occupy Wall Street?

Jennifer: A series of things. First of all, the economy needs to be fixed. Jobs should be readily available. People should be able to leave the homeless shelters within six months, maybe less. They need to concentrate on the fact that people are poor even if they are employed.

Hannah Faye: Would you be out here if you had a job?

Jennifer: That's a very interesting question. And I'm just going to be straight forward with you. If I had a job and I was working I wouldn't be out here everyday. I definitely wouldn't be out here in this weather. If the weather was like this, no; if the weather wasn't like this, yes I would. If I had a job I wouldn't be out here as frequently because maybe I would have an apartment too.

Hannah Faye: What is your message to people who don't care about this event?

Jennifer: You need to wake up. Please take this seriously because this is not a joke. Thirdly, learn some things about it. Learn about Occupy Wall Street if you don't know about it. Hang around informative people.

Hannah Faye: What do you say to people who totally disagree with the whole idea?

Jennifer: First of all those people are full of a bunch of crap, shit whatever you want to call it, piss, mess...and those are the people that we need help from. I feel like we are robots controlled by the government. We just haven't had the mark of the beast yet. You know like the sixes or something like that. I feel like they don't give a fuck, they don't care, whatever you want to call it. It's not them. It's not their family. They don't care. They are greedy for money. They need to be out here to see what it feels like. Maybe they'll wake up and do some inventory on themselves.

Hannah Faye: Final words?

Jennifer: Be strong. That's the first thing I can say. Don't give up. That's the second thing. And the third thing is it's either going to get better or it's going to get worse. Together we stand, divided we fall. I think the message is getting out there and in some cases the media is showing like negative things about the movement. It's mixed messages. You can take it for what it's worth and what good is being done. Or you can see what negative things are being done. You can take both in stride. But that's not what the movement is about. It's not about negativity. It's about people sticking together as one and helping each other out as one. It's about coming together as one and fighting against what they call a democracy. It's about going after these animals, these higher ups in office. It's about change. The movement is about change.

Hannah Faye: Who do you represent? Do you want to represent just yourself or a group of people?

Jennifer: Well, I'm representing primarily LGBT, a group for Lesbian, Gay, Bi-Sexual and Transgender people, mainly the ones who are 30 and older.

Hannah Faye: Are you transgender?

Jennifer: Yes I am.

Hannah Faye: Do you mind if I mention that in the book?

Jennifer: It's okay.

Hannah Faye: I think that's important. Do you have anything else you'd like to say?

Jennifer: No. I think that's it.

19

Josef, 49

Date: Saturday, October 29, 2011
Location: Wall Street, New York
Event: Occupy Wall Street
Occupation: Pastor
Transcribed Voice Recording

Hannah Faye: I'm here at the Occupy Wall Street movement in New York, NY sitting across from Josef. Josef is a non-participant in the movement however he is a supporter of the movement. Josef, where are you from?

Josef: I'm originally from Germany, but I live in Pennsylvania.

Hannah Faye: Why are you here?

Josef: I'm here because I want to be a voice for the Church. I believe that Jesus, who walked on the earth, who was someone who identified with the poor, would not condone the kind of greed that this nation condones. I just want to be a voice and the hands and feet of the one I believe in, the one who said he takes care of those who are weak and meek (Jesus). I want to be a living demonstration of that. I want to make my voice known and the voice which belongs to the church.

Hannah Faye: When did you decide this wasn't an event to just to watch on T.V. but something to experience physically in person?

Josef: There were some friends of mine who felt the same way I did. We felt we needed to support this movement. So I joined a few friends and we came here together while enjoying the fellowship of each other. It encourages us to be faithful in what we believe in. I understand that some people may feel this is just another movement and don't necessarily want to identify with that. I think I can relate to people who may get a little phlegmatic about the needs of others. There are so many needs, we see them on the internet and on T.V. and sometimes it can get a little overwhelming. So I think it's easy to say this is just another movement. It's easy to excuse them (the protesters). So I can understand from my own experience. That's an easy thing to do. I do think, by and large people are caring and supportive of those who are in need, but as a Christian I think I need to go beyond what most people would do. I think Jesus transforms lives. And as someone who has been touched by the love and mercy of Jesus I want to be an expression of that and go through some snow and some rain to demonstrate that. I think as a German citizen also, as an outsider to this country, I just want to encourage this population seriously. Due to the need, I think it would help us all (in the world) if we would be willing to share what we have. I understand that not everyone shares the same faith, but I think as human beings we can still share the same sentiment of what it would be like to be in need. We need to take responsibility for one another.

Hannah Faye: Thank you Josef. Is there anything else you'd like to add?

Josef: I appreciate people like you (Hannah Faye) who take this seriously and maybe who are helping the movement to be known by publishing things. I think that's how this thing has gotten traction. It's the normal people who are in the streets, who need to be taken seriously; not the ones who necessarily have the power or the money to perpetrate their issues.

20

Supporters and the 1%

On Saturday, October 29, 2011 I saw many people like Josef in the previous chapter. They are non-participants in the movement itself, but are in fact supporters: people who are not actively involved in protesting, but are helping to sustain the movement. This support ranges from simply attending assemblies to donating goods to demonstrators. On this day I watched as many supporters brought bags of clothing, food and other supplies to the Comfort station. They thanked the protesters for their courage before departing. However when I asked one of them for an interview she declined stating she would love to but that she may risk losing her job. When I assured her she could use a pseudonym she encouraged me further to interview someone else.

My heart goes out to supporters. After speaking with Josef, I considered the hard place they might be in. Many supporters, like this woman above are living their full lives. Perhaps they are apart of the 99%, but they are in the middle-upper class 99%. They don't have any needs because they are all being met by their good salaries. They have good jobs, nice homes, healthcare, etc. Their hearts tell them to stand with the 99%, but they are afraid of losing the security they've worked their whole lives to acquire. They agree with nearly everything the 99ers are saying, but they feel it's only so much they can do. Perhaps, it's hard for them to understand how much they have been effected by the corporate world. Perhaps, it's hard for them to take back the control; especially when they feel the corporate world has given them so much. The hard truth is that the corporate world has mentally crippled them in such a way that they feel like they can't even be true to themselves. They are disabled from being true activists.

And then you have the supporters who *are* in the 1%. You might not think so, but many of them feel the same way everyone else does. Although I was unable to interview any of them personally, I do know they've given hundreds of thousands of dollars anonymously for the cause. They want change just as much as the protesters do. However, some are like the middle-upper classmen in this aspect. They will only do so much before backing off. They enjoy their trips to Cancun, Hawaii, Paris and other exotic places all over the globe. You try giving up your Bentley in exchange for a Honda. You try giving up your fifteen room mansion for a two bedroom apartment, especially when you feel like you've worked so hard for the former. Try slicing your filet mignon in half for a hamburger from Wendy's. They are more nervous than ever because they feel like they are being asked to give these pleasures up. They understand poverty, they understand how bad the economy is, but they are nervous about losing everything they have too. They are driven by their desire to acquire more and more and if you know anything about success, you know it is addictive. Perhaps many of them feel like 99% of the world is now trying to take that success away from them. But any one percenter who thinks this should look closer into the cause and understand this is not the goal of the 99%. From my understanding, they do not want the one percent's Bentleys. They do not want the Lexuses. They do not want the one percent's idea of success. The 99% want an equal society where everyone is able to achieve success and freedom, whatever that may be for any individual across this world. And I don't know anyone in their right minds who would be against that. Considering this, it is the author's opinion that the classes must find a way to compromise with one another. They must meet eye to eye. In order for this to take place the 1% must lower themselves to the 99%. And the 99% must give the 1% the benefit of the doubt. After all, aren't we all a part of the 100%?

21

Jordan Eck, 20

Date: Saturday, October 29, 2011
Location: Wall Street, New York
Event: Occupy Wall Street
Transcribed Voice Recording

I'm definitely a participant. This is my 29th day here. The reason why I'm here in regards to the movement...I want to support the movement however I can. In terms of why that's important...I think it's crucial that we spend as much energy as we can trying to raise awareness of how bad this situation really is in this country and as far as what our country has done to the world. I want people to look into it for themselves and realize corporations have way too much influence on the government. They are making choices that are detrimental to the rest of the world and our citizens here. I feel like by being here we are making people talk about it. Hopefully, that's made a lot of people look into the facts and doing that has helped them to see that our government, the U.S. government is making policies, laws and regulations that don't benefit us and especially don't benefit people in third world countries, but instead benefit huge corporations in terms of environmental degradation. They are screwing up our environment and a lot of human rights. People have been killed by death squads just so we (U.S.) can gain access to their resources...Exxon Mobile, all sorts of various corporations. I feel like the act of being out here isn't as important as people knowing about it...seeing and looking into it. I feel like if they did know they'd be just as mad as all of us are out here. People say that we don't have a coherent and all-encompassing message, but the issue with that is that there's so much shit that's wrong in the world. There's so much trouble that's being caused by this corporate influence that you can't encompass that in one, single demand or one, single message because corporations are screwing us all over. I want to support it so that it can last for as long as it can because the longer we last, the more people find out, the more people are going to look into it and ask why are these people out here in the park while it's snowing (laughs) and cold and wet. Like, I have a wonderful, awesome home that I could stay in and be warm in. But I feel like, as a Christian I can't do that. It's important for me to really spread social justice as much as I can. And I feel like the most expedient means of doing that is raising social awareness. Without people power we can't change this system. I hope that we can change this system. I'm hoping that power hasn't been concentrated so much that we're in an oligarchy for life or we're heading towards a fascist state. That's why we're (protesters) here. We're trying to prevent the manipulation and the taking away of the voices of the people and replacing them with the voices of the powerful. I mean, I don't know all of the facts, but I feel like anybody who knew the majority of the facts would be pissed. You can't not be pissed when you see a village in El Salvador being massacred by our armies or armies we've created for the sake of corporate interests. They (El Salvador) don't deserve that. They have just as much right to be happy as we do and I just don't think it's right. I know for a fact it's not right and I want to do something about it. I feel like I can't be content in life unless I make an effort. As of right now, in this country that effort is Occupy Wall Street. That's why I'm here. And I'm going to stick it out. I'm going to be here through the winter. I'm going to be here as long as I can. Of course the corporate media...they'll do what they can to lessen our message. They'll talk about our camp and little trivial things that don't matter while completely ignoring the reasons we're out here. But a little bit of truth will get through and that's what's important. We need that little bit to get through. We're not crazy. We're not anarchists. We're reasonable. We've looked at the facts. We know for a fact that things aren't right and that's indisputable at this point. People need to take an unbiased look and let go of their preconceived notions and understand that people are being hurt. Perhaps they themselves are not in that situation and neither am I. I mean, I have one of the best lives that you can imagine. I was born in America, I have an amazing quality of life, but the vast majority of people don't. They don't even come close and it's because of corporations...and not just corporations, but people are screwing us over. You have to look at it and understand it's about all of us. It's not just about you. Even if you're alright a lot of people aren't and no one can dispute that and here are the reasons. America has so much power and influence we could eradicate poverty. We could fix this world or at least come a lot closer than we are but instead we're going in the opposite direction and that's not a country that I want to be apart of. I mean, I'm so proud to be an American, but when it comes to our government...I have a lot of problems with it. This is going to sound so cliché and like your average hippy sentiment, but this is really all about love. You're never going to be happy unless you start going beyond your own personal contentment and you start looking around. Everyone wants exactly what you want. They just want to be content. They just want to be happy. You're going to be a lot happier when you start putting effort towards making others happy as well as yourself. So give that some thought and priority because it'll benefit your life as well.

22

"Sinister"

Date: Saturday, October 29, 2011
Location: Wall Street, New York
Event: Occupy Wall Street
Age: 29
Occupation: Unemployed
Transcribed Voice Recording

First of all, I want to say God bless everybody. The reason why I'm here is in two reasons: unity and equality. I believe that if we live in the United States we should be united and have equal rights. That's what I'm here for. And sense I've been here I've been mingling and networking with people from all walks of life. I've been talking to people I wouldn't normally be talking to, including the author (Hannah Faye). The first time I stepped foot down here I felt like I was obligated to spend the night with the people. So I spent the night with the people and I woke up and I felt one with the people. I felt good. And when I woke up I found $20 and I just spent it with the people. Usually I would've went and got some other stuff just for myself, but I just feel like I'm one with the people now so I shared it. I'm not saying this is a revolution, but we're off to a big start. I've been down here for two weeks. I'm here for unity and equality. I don't believe those are things we should have to fight for. I believe these things should come naturally to all people. To me, this is really not a fight. A lot of people are still asleep, selfish...as long as they have their jobs, as long as they have roofs over their heads, they're good. But they're not thinking about their kids or their grandkids. What we're protesting about here we may never live to see the change. It may not be for us. It's for our kids. Everyone has a right to continue living life as they are now. They have a right to be that way. It's sad that, at the end of the day if we (the protesters) do accomplish something their kids will reap the rewards even though they weren't out here protesting and may have even been against the protesting altogether (laughs). You feel me? It's sad that it might end up that way. However, what can you do? Even though they are selfish at least we made a change for their kids. So either way the impact is going to hit someone directly or indirectly.

Hannah Faye: Final words?

Sinister: As long as people go out and get this book *(Occupy the World: From the Heart of the Protesters)* it really doesn't matter about me (laughs) or what I think. At the end of the day everybody is their own person. But if you hear me or if you read this book it's going to hit you directly or indirectly. If not, it's going to hit someone that's close to you. You feel me? Just imagine waking up in a world that's a better place for you and your kids. That's the future. That's all I got to say.

23

"Marcell"

Date: Saturday, October 29, 2011
Location: Wall Street, New York
Event: Occupy Wall Street
Age: 23
Transcribed Voice Recording

I'm participating in such a way that I'm here but I'm not really protesting. I'm here because I was led by the Holy Spirit of God to give a testimony of Jesus Christ of all the things that I've seen in my life and to show that Jesus Christ is real and that everything that happened in prophecy speaking of him is true. He rose from the dead. John 3:16 says for God so loved the world that he sent his only begotten son that whosoever believed in him should not perish. I'm here to testify of those things...that he is true. And whoever hears my testimony and takes heed to those things will be blessed, but those who turn away will perish. That's why I'm here. This is how the Holy Spirit leads me by prophecies, in dreams, signs and visions after I've prayed and been obedient to God through the Holy Spirit and through Jesus Christ. I've had signs and visions of things that he brought to life in reality and I have no choice but to follow. It all leads me here to Wall Street. In the prophecy it showed me this is where I was supposed to be. I've been here in New York since August 1st. There was a little bit going on when I got here, but I didn't know how wide it was going to spread. As far as the location, which is Liberty Street and Broadway, they weren't here yet when I first came. They were still on the actual Wall Street. It took me a while to understand that where they are right now, that's where God wanted me to be. But I was already prompted to be apart of this before I got to New York. I already knew what it was that God wanted me to do. I just didn't know exactly where he wanted me to be. Now that this is going on and I refer back to the prophecy...and I really can't say too much about the vision but there was a time in tribulation where I had to overcome Satan. Even in the prophecy...in Winston Salem, N.C. where I'm from, this is where the dream took place. There was a time of tribulation where I had to overcome the devil. It took place on a street called Liberty Street back in N.C. and now I'm here on Liberty Street and I see what's going on here, where the people feel like they're being shorthanded. The thing that they (protesters) want...people don't really understand the thing that they're asking for. It's not too much I can say about what's about to take place here because me, myself, I don't know for sure. Only God knows and I don't want to say anything that would mislead anybody. I'm only going to say why I'm here. I'm here to testify about Jesus Christ, that he is real and God did raise him on the third day. Basically, what God is saying is that only through Christ can you come to him. Those who reject God, they shall perish. I believe all of this is leading to the rise of the Anti-Christ and the false messiah which everybody is really waiting for. Whether it is a system of people or a person or a few people...they are going to give false peace and false hope. And after that comes the tribulation. A lot of people are going to fall for this. As far as the money system goes, if you look around, you hear what a lot of people are saying. They're saying that currency is causing all the greed and the destruction. What I'm seeing is that they want to come up with a system where you don't need money. And when you look at that it goes back to taking on the mark of the beast, which people don't believe is real. I see what's going on right now and I think about John the Baptist, who lead the way for the true Messiah...a lot of things that are going on right now are leading the way for the false messiah which is the devil himself, who comes to the world to deceive many people. If anyone follows him they shall perish. Until then there's not much I can say. Whoever reads the book (Occupy the World: From the Heart of the Protesters) and wants to ask me of my full testimony, I can give it to them. I can tell them everything that happened in my life which cannot be explained scientifically. At the time these things occurred I had no choice but to believe that it was the true Creator doing these things in my life. As I was growing up I didn't know what everything meant until God revealed everything to me and showed me this is what it is. It's good to take heed to the things that I say because these things (signs and visions) really took place in my life and they all point back to Jesus Christ as Lord and Savior. He was the one who walked with me. I actually walked with him and it was such a sad thing because it blew my mind. Even I had doubts. But after he showed me everything I have no doubts. Take heed. That's all I can say. I represent the Lord and Savior Jesus Christ. In order for me to do this I had to give up all of my desires. I had to give up wanting to be successful for myself. Now if I represent myself I'm representing a sinner who basically did a lot of wrongs. My name is not worthy of anything. I came to represent the name that is worthy before the father in heaven, which is Jesus Christ, the one he sent by which we shall be saved. That's who I represent. John 3:16 is the easiest thing to remember when it comes to what God gave mankind. In Revelation it says he who is obedient...to those who are obedient he (God) will reveal himself to them. Now there were some times in my life when I was without sin. These were the times when I saw the things (signs and visions). These were the times when God came and spoke to me...when I was without sin and when I was being obedient. He gave me the testimony to give to you (Hannah Faye). To those who don't believe and haven't seen anything...the reason why you haven't seen anything is because you didn't believe from the start. And if you would've believed from the start then you would've obeyed because you would understand there was one above you watching the things that you did. But sense you didn't believe and you didn't care about his (God's) law you didn't do anything he required you to do. And this is not to boast of anything. I just happened to be a person who obeyed the things that he said. And by me believing and really having faith that he was there he showed me things. But if you do not obey his will you will not have any connection with him whatsoever. The only connection you can have with God is simply the breath that is given from him to you to keep you alive until he decides to take his mercy from you and that is when you die. That is your only connection with God. Other than that, you will see nothing. It (the bible) says anyone who doubts, they can expect nothing from the father in heaven. Whatever you ask of him you shall receive. Jesus said whatsoever you ask the father in my name you will receive, but anyone who has doubt you can expect nothing from the father. The first step is to believe that he is there. If you believe that he is there and you believe in what he says that is what will cause you to be right. But for those who don't believe he's there...they have nothing to motivate them to follow the laws of God.

That's why they see nothing. Everything will be revealed about the spirits that live inside of people. There are only two sides to this whole thing. In this world, you have good and you have evil. It's just hard to explain because before you can grasp the whole thing you have to actually be a child. Those who didn't grasp it from the start...they are not children of God. They are children of the devil because they followed him. It's the same with all the angels...the great number of them that followed the devil. Now, my message to those who refuse to believe is this here...anyone denying that Jesus Christ is the Son of God is anti-Christ. That means you're against everything that is of the Christ. You don't agree that God sent the Christ. But you have to wake up and look at what's in front of you. As far as me speaking, Hannah...I can talk until I turn blue but the thing that God gave me to give to the world is my testimony. A lot of times when I try to give my testimony...these words that I'm saying right now they're not going to bring anybody to the light. I want to tell the things that happened in my life and to show the truth. These things (signs and visions) really took place in my life. Now, the devil knows these things. And since Jesus died and rose from the dead, since that day it's been shown in the book (the bible) that those who follow Satan, they feared what would happen because they knew that if the message of Jesus' death went around the whole world and people believed it, they knew they would lose their power in the world. The reason they try to keep the message from you is because they want to keep the power, they want to keep holding the world because they themselves didn't believe from the start. They have been doomed from the start. So to all who don't believe they're going to fall under that same thing. And as of right now, I really feel like God wants me to stop because it's not too much I can say. And for me to give my testimony on this (recorder) right here, it would take forever. I already had plans before this interview began and I want to write all these things down. I feel like if I just tell little stories here and there about the things that happened it's going to leave a lot of room for questioning. And I want to have it to where there's no room for questioning. It's my testimony. It's what God trusted me with. I have a choice of what I want to do with it. I can either bury it and keep it from the people or I can expose it to the best of my ability. And what I want to do is expose it to the best of my ability. If I just give little pieces of it people are going to ask questions and I want people to be able to see it in full. Some people are going to doubt it no matter what and some people are going to take it. I've been dealing with that sense I've been here in New York. I mean, God told me he was going to send me to a hardheaded people. New York is so hardheaded. Like, back where I'm from (Winston Salem, N.C.) people received my message and they received it gladly. Some people rejected it, but most received it gladly. I believe that, through me a few souls were saved, but here in New York...it's like this is the world of darkness up here. It's so many people...and the spirit of evil is up here so thick. The people that are thick minded and don't want to hear it...I guess these people have been through so much in their life they have the same question I used to have when I was an atheist: if God is real how come these things have happened? But one thing you have to understand is that the devil is real also. These are my final words right here: God is merciful. He gave you the easiest thing to do. He knows we're going to break his law. He knows that we cannot follow the Ten Commandments throughout our lives. That's why he gave us the blood which is his sacrifice sent to the world. For God so loved the world that he gave his only begotten son that whosoever believeth in him shall not perish but have everlasting life. Once you receive Jesus Christ as your Lord and Savior, his blood that was shed at cavalry washes away all of your sins in front of the father. By believing in him it makes you righteous...just by believing that this is the true way. Your sins are covered by the blood. If you do not take this covering, if you do not receive God's sacrifice...you have to understand...man is made out of God's image and from his likeness. We're not supposed to just look like him, but we're supposed to think and act like him. Even back to the beginning of time seeing how Cain was and how he didn't receive his sacrifice. Cain was angry with God. It caused jealousy and he ended up killing Abel. But first, Cain was angry with God. So if we're made in God's image and made to be like him how do you think God feels about you not receiving his sacrifice which was the lamb, Jesus Christ? He sent him for his blood to be shed for us. You have to understand that. That's all I want to say for now. I don't know what God's going to do. I don't know the future. Sometimes he tells me to do things and I don't understand why I'm doing it until it's over, but I will say this...my name is Leondris Jeffreys. I go by Marcell. If you hear of my name this is not for any representation and not for any fame, but it's simply for the testimony of Jesus Christ. I beg and plead with you to take heed to everything I've said to you. Please take heed because these are true things. The things that happened in the bible are not fables. They really happened so take heed.

24

Khorey Rice, 17

Date: Saturday, October 29, 2011
Location: Wall Street, New York
Event: Occupy Wall Street
Transcribed Voice Recording

I'm a participant in the Occupy Wall Street movement. I've been coming since the 22nd of September. On the 22nd there was a Troy Davis protest all the way from Spring Street to Wall Street. So I stopped and started listening to what the protesters (Occupy Wall Street) were talking about at the general assembly and I felt like I could help out in some way. I started out during security. Then I went on to helping out with the media. But recently, in the last week we've been getting a lot of bad attention. There have been a lot of drunken people walking around. But I see us growing. Even in the cold weather...I mean a lot of things have put us down at this point, but I feel like in the future we're going to get a lot stronger. We've died down a little bit. People come and go. Thugs are getting arrested...I mean we're getting punched from everywhere. The weather is punching us. Even the police...like recently just the other day I was a victim of the police blowing something totally out of proportion. There was a fight in the park and it was video recorded. I just happened to be on the tape and they put me on Fox 5 news claiming they were looking for me. They're trying to throw anything and everything at us at this point and that just shows we're getting strong. They're trying to hurt us so that proves we're strong. I just hope it keeps going. I'm going to be here until the end, you know what I'm saying. I don't want to just say that I'm here fighting for one thing. But I feel like the reason I'm here is because we have to start somewhere. It's better to do it than not to do it. I feel like change is pretty close. I know it's close. I mean, look around. People are suffering all over the world. Something's got to change. Stand up and fight for your rights! If you don't do it what are you going to do for yourself? What would happen if the stock market crashed? What would you do? I'm not going to lie, it probably is a lot of crazies out here now, but there are also some people who really put their lives on the line for this protest. There are people who sleep here. They're here 24/7 helping us. They're why we've come so far. I think it started off with like 20 people sleeping here and now it's like 80 people that sleep here at night and like 20,000 people here during the day. We're strong. We get some blows from everywhere but we're not going to fold.

Hannah Faye: Man, you are seventeen years old?

Khorey: Right.

Hannah Faye: You are the youngest person I've interviewed. What do you say to people who are your age and younger?

Khorey: Do something that'll help the world and yourself. I'm not going to say come to *Occupy Wall Street* for somebody else's cause because this may not be their cause, but really just fight for whatever you need in the world...whatever you see as good...fight for that.

Hannah Faye: Do your parents know you're down here?

Khorey: Yes, they do.

Hannah Faye: How do they feel?

Khorey: They say don't get locked up (laughs).

Hannah Faye: Final words?

Khorey: This is the start of us building a better country. Forget all the rumors about the New World Order and all that. This is the start of the people building a country we want to live in.

25

Tyrone Dickerson

Date: Saturday, October 29, 2011
Location: Wall Street, New York
Event: Occupy Wall Street
Transcribed Voice Recording

I'm here because in the seventh grade I realized the fix was in. I was given tests...we were tested every Friday, but I wasn't learning anything. So I went to my teacher Mrs. V and I said: Why don't you address the students and have a piece about how the fix is in and how these people are supposed to be less educated than everyone else and how they're not supposed to receive the same education as everyone else. I asked her why she didn't address that. I was the only one in my entire seventh grade class, who thought like this. I was the only one with enough courage to ask the teacher these things. I was ridiculed because of it and for things like that in school. So that's why I'm here. I knew the fix was in. I saw it. Now I finally get to do something about it. I'm also here because of my education. I know that 1% owns 40% of the world's wealth. I know that 50% of all Americans make less than $24,000 a year, which is a joke. I know that there are one billion people in poverty right now, which is a joke. If it was a hundred million people that would be a joke; if it was five hundred million people in poverty that would be a joke...one billion? That's unimaginable. I know that the founding fathers were actually ahead of their time and planned this whole thing out. They actually planned this out. This system has been going on for 200 years and this is all going according to plan. The problem is the income has reached a point to where it's so great that it's visible now. You don't even need education to see it. You can just walk outside and see the homeless people and see that something's not right. There are more homeless people. I know that since 1979 to 2009 the disparity has increased. It's ridiculous. I used to believe that the drug war...the people who were involved in it were scum bags. But now, I understand it. It's a war on poverty...the people in poverty. It's a war on the middle class that has been put in place by the 1%. I'm also here because of the corporation take over of music, namely rap music...presenting rap artists with guns, talking about "bitches and hoes." They're keeping people down on that level. And they're not just using rap music. You got Lady Gaga. They're using people like this to represent all this garbage...Justin Bieber. Lil' Wayne could make a rap song right now with a good beat saying the corporations are killing us, but he won't do that. They could get kids to memorize stuff like that. But no, they (rap artists) don't do that. What do they say? "Bitches, hoes, guns" and talk about this and that. Why else am I here? I'm here because I was a Human Services major and I always wanted to help people as a kid. That's when I figured all this stuff out. I decided a long time ago that something wasn't right. What are some other stats? The unemployment rate is 9.1% right now. By next September they project it to be 18.4%. In the black community right now it's projected to be 25.4%. This is a joke. If a black person kills a white person their sixteen times more likely to get the death penalty than if a white person kills a black person. Forty percent of all black children are living in poverty right now. This is a joke. The last four presidents have smoked marijuana and they've risen to presidency. But you get normal people out here smoking marijuana and they're getting summoned, but the presidents are doing it and nothing is happening to them. It all starts with the founding fathers. The constitution...it all started from there. Those people were ahead of their time. I'm impressed. I'm impressed that the 1% has distorted these people's minds so bad they don't really know what's going on. Even with religion...I'm impressed. They've figured out a way for people to believe in an imaginary friend to feel comfortable with them selves to make them think nothing matters right now because when they die they're good. They're going to be living the life in heaven. What a joke! No one has ever come back from heaven and explained that. You know? I'm impressed. That's why I'm down here. Another reason why I'm here...the money in politics has gotten out of hand. In Obama's last campaign he was funded $76 million dollars. That is the most money any politician has earned in the history of campaigning. I'm kind of an Obama fan but I'm also not an idiot. I know if someone gives you $76 million dollars and puts you in position you must go back to that person and say thank you and see what you can do for them. And these people who gave him the funds are in the 1%. Who else would they be? No one else has that kind of money. So the 1% are pushing their agendas through politicians. I realized a long time ago that the 1% use the police as dogs to go after the 99%. It's a joke. I'm also here because of the patriot act that was passed by George Bush, which is the biggest joke in American history. They've been looking at your e-mails; they've been looking at your phone records. That's why when I was in college for two years I would send myself the U.S. constitution, just hoping that they would read it going through my e-mails. It's so stupid. I know about all of the big fixes that are going on. I watch the news all the time and they're always asking what do they (the protesters) want, what's the one thing they want. Well, I just named several things. Another reason why I'm down here is because of the Republicans, the 1%. They have signed pledges not to be taxed anymore. That has never happened in the history of this country where they just said: nope, we're not getting taxed anymore. We're done with being taxed. They're taxed at 33% now, well really 18% with the loop holes. And Obama's job plan is going to increase that to 36%. What a joke. Under Eisenhower, the rich paid 78% on taxes and they were still rich. They need to pay for what they've done. Put them at 88%. Put them at least at 78%. That's a big reason why I'm here...the taxes. The corporations have taken over every area of our lives. Not to be crude, but they have taken us by the balls. They control what we watch which makes up our opinions. They control what we eat which effects our lifespan. They control what we listen to and they control our level of intelligence. Recently, since I've come back to the Bronx, I see people walking down the street screaming out rap lyrics at the top of their lungs. That's a problem. It's so bad that it's gotten to a schizophrenic level. It's impressive the system the 1% has created. You have to be extremely intelligent to create a system that works for 200 years without anyone bringing it up. The pharmaceutical companies...they have a lobby...they push medicine through that kills people. You take this medicine, you get a headache because of it and then you have to take another medicine. So now you have to take two pills and on and on and on. Corporations have taken over food. Look, we're sitting in

McDonald's right now. You can buy a sandwich for $1 and it's killing you. I used to work as a manager for McDonald's. I know exactly what's in the food. Then when I quit and decided I wanted to get a real job with benefits I looked and there weren't any around. I'm stuck just like everyone else. Everyone else is here for those reasons but some of them can't articulate that. But they have instincts. They can feel that something is wrong. They don't know exactly what's wrong, but they can feel it. And I encourage you to be selective in who you interview for this book project because some of these people are not down here for the movement. Some of them have just come down here in the last two weeks. I've been here for four weeks and these people are smoking cigs, sitting in McDonald's, eating free food at the park, then smoking more cigs, listening to the drums and then going to bed. And they're doing the same things everyday. They're not in any working groups, they're not on any committees, they're not doing any direct action, they're not in the general assembly, and they're not doing anything constructive with their time. They're smoking cigs...I mean they can do that. This is a free country...but you have to do things (within the movement). There are people taking advantage of the freedoms here. We (the protesters) knew this was going to happen. We knew once we gave out free tents, free food...that the ex-cons, the crazies, the scavengers and the squatters were going to come down. Even some of the 1% come down here on their lunch breaks and eat the food. Then they take some pictures, dance to the drums and leave. Maybe by coming down here it makes them sleep better at night. But you're not giving me healthcare and I'm feeding you? No way. So we've put together a plan where we're not going to give out the gourmet food anymore from the kitchen. We're going to give you peanut butter and jelly on stale bread. Now it's snowing and you're going to leave because you're going to get cold and you're going to go into a shelter or you're going to go home. Some of these people say they're out here for change, but I think they're out here literally for change (money). The last three days I've been hearing a lot of people asking about where the money is going. We got $435,000 donated to us from anonymous sources. I mean, we know who's giving it. It's regular celebrities and people who've come down here every day to give. Last week, Russell Simmons came down here literally every day and donated coats, tents, food, etc. Kanye West was actually down here this morning and he was here before. He came down here with a three million dollar suit on. What a joke! I don't know what he was wearing today. People from Fox5 news have been down here. Michael Moore's been down here. He's been supported. I saw Jesse Jackson. I actually conversated with Jesse Jackson. I like Jesse. He's a professional protester. He knows how to do it. But I've got people asking me where all this money is going. It's because they want some money, but they're not doing any kind of direct action to get it. They're not doing anything. They don't deserve any money. Now, if you want to start a working campaign we can give you $100 a day. That's for transportation, flyers, and whatever you need. But they don't want to do that. They want to sit around and smoke cigs. They want to get paid to smoke cigs and eat food. Some of these people are a joke. I remember putting blankets on homeless people. They wouldn't ask me to do it...I would just do it. Now I may see them and walk right over them. I've seen the evolution of this movement. We are in the process of weaning these lazy people out. This is the first day. The weather is going to do it. The food is going to do it. We're on the right track right now. I mean, look around. People are in this McDonald's...but people die everyday from McDonald's. Another reason why I'm here is because of the hypocrisy that reigns throughout this country. This country wasn't supposed to be like that. And the people who are out here just sitting around and complaining...those are the ones who are out of the loop. They're not apart of the organization because they're not doing any action. It's disappointing. I'm disappointed in a lot of these people. Like, my generation...the 18-30 year olds...we're the ones that have woken up and are actually trying to do something. Older people are so delusional. You don't see a lot of older minorities down here. My parents are not down here because this (system) is what they feel God wants for them, but religion...religion was created by the 1% and it worked so well. We're going to be down here at least until 2016. I'm hoping that by 2016 we'll have four political choices. We'll have the tea party candidate, a republican candidate, a democrat, and a 99er. We're creating a 99% caucus right now. I'm apart of Direct Action and General Assembly. We're doing a 99 caucus and we're putting together a 99 party and we won't lose because we're too big to fail. It's 99% of us. So we will never lose an election. Another goal of mine is to get rid of the Electoral College. What a joke that is! You have swing states where candidates only go to Iowa and Florida and the other states don't matter as much. Another thing is health...the elected officials and important people don't care about the people's health at all. Hillary Clinton's healthcare plan had the word *Nutrition* in it once. It had the word *Exercise* in it once, the words *Pharmaceutical* and *Pills* came up over 200 times. How are you getting healthy off of pills? You stay healthy from nutrition and exercise. So when we have a 99% group that's not corporate funded than we can actually push our stuff through and we will not lose.

Hannah Faye: A little off topic here, what is your opinion of the idea that there may be a billionaire somewhere orchestrating this whole thing?

Tyrone: A billionaire funding this whole thing? I would be supportive of a billionaire supporting this (laughs).

Hannah Faye: Are there people making money off of this event?

Tyrone: Yes. There are people already selling pens, people selling marijuana, etc. People are selling pens that say *99%* on them. Merchants are actually banking off of this. You know, they got $5 pens. They're using capitalism. They're using the system that we're (protesters) supposed to be going against. But they're doing it in many other different ways. It's not just that. The 99% (protesters)...we're against McDonald's because we're against poisoning people. But there's so called protesters in here eating McDonald's. They're contradicting themselves. That's why I told you to be selective in who you choose to interview. Some of these people haven't taken the time to educate themselves. They don't care. They think it's a big party down here. Halloween is coming up and they want to hang out. It's like High School Part 2. It's like High School....people are hanging out, talking to one another, eating, and sleeping together. These kinds of people are not out here for the right reasons.

*At this point Rhachi from a previous chapter (See Chapter 15) approaches us and begins discussing his inclusion in my book project. Rhachi and Tyrone then indistinctly discuss a rap artist named Jay-Z. Rhachi shares with us that Jay-Z has taught him a lot about life, but Tyrone disagrees stating that Jay-Z's music is controlled by corporations which only help to distort people's minds. After Rhachi shares a quote from one of Jay-Z's songs, Tyrone replies:

I know a Jay-Z quote that's awesome (sarcastically) that has brainwashed and destroyed kids' minds. It's the chorus to one of his songs and it plays three times: "Money, cash, hoes, money, cash, hoes." When that's the chorus to one of your songs that's a problem. And the corporations are behind it. They are pushing that. If you go against the grain and you make a rap song that the corporations are trying to brainwash us and you put that into your chorus, that's not going to be played. They're on the news, they're on the radio stations and many of them own the record labels. Roc-Nation is a corporation. Jay-Z is a lot of people's hero. It's a joke.

Hannah Faye: Final words?

Tyrone: Research. Be aware and be informed. Stop being delusional! I was one of the people who were delusional for a long time. The best thing you can do in life is to ask why. Why am I listening to this (music) everyday? Why do I know so much about Lebron James and Michael Jordan? Why do I know how many threes Michael Jordan hit in his career, but I don't know how the branches of government work. I don't know about the constitution. I don't know any amendments. I don't know who's funding which politicians. I don't know how healthcare works. I mean, *I* know. But people (in general) don't know. Why don't I know how the global economy works? Why don't I know about the loop holes? But I know all the rap lyrics. I know when a certain song came out. I know all about sports...useless information. But why don't people know the real information? Some of this stuff people should be able to pick up from just being alive, but they don't. They ignore it. And the thing is, it all starts with school. They are purposefully not teaching these kids what they need to know. Why can't they just be honest and say that? That would've awakened us. But they (teachers) won't say that. And these are people who have their PhDs and Masters and all that. They're very smart, but they don't want us to be. They get the test and they teach to the test. It's a joke. I saw an article yesterday that only 25% of New York seniors are ready for college. That's why I'm out here. There are just too many jokes going on for one comedy club.

26

Tommy, 19

Date: Saturday, October 29, 2011
Location: Wall Street, New York
Event: Occupy Wall Street
Occupation: Student
Written Response

I'm with the New York branch of the Party for Socialism and Liberation. As an active member it is my duty to be here at Occupy Wall Street. History has shown us that this system of capitalism has done nothing but benefit a tiny minority of wealthy individuals while benefiting a few. The majority of working class families are being pushed further and further into despair. But we must understand that this is not just because capitalism was corrupted. This is the inherent nature of capitalism which thrives on profit. If this system only expands because of profit then there is no wonder why we see the injustices we see everyday such as: sexism, racism and anti-lesbian, gay, bi-sexual and transgender bigotry amongst the countless other injustices we see everyday in our community. We must understand that these things are not because of flaws in human nature, but instead the necessities that make capitalism expand. These things keep us in competition with one another as diligent workers while binding us from our true oppressors: capitalism and the capitalists that benefit off of the backs of our miseries. It's funny how under the disguise of humanitarian intervention they can make record profits, exploiting Iraq, Afghanistan, Haiti and Libya. But we know damn well that there's no humanitarian intervention in one million Iraqi civilians murdered in 10 years. There's no humanitarian intervention in drones being dropped on Libyan school children with no hopes for tomorrow. And there sure as hell ain't no humanitarian intervention in our schools being shut down, workers being laid off and various other social programs being cut. Reform will just delay our demise. A new society is necessary and the only way that comes is by Revolution.

27

Kerbie Joseph, 23

Date: Saturday, October 29, 2011
Location: Wall Street, New York
Event: Occupy Wall Street
Occupation: Student
Transcribed Voice Recording

I've been an activist for most of my college career, every since I was about 20. One thing that I learned about was the power of my voice. I have a Caribbean background. My mom is a hardworking woman. She came from Haiti, worked in a factory and now she is a home-health aide. She's 65 years old and works several hours a day. Retirement is no where in sight for her. With that type of background, growing up in Brooklyn, which is not the best place to live in terms of poverty. I was taught to keep my head down and not use my voice. It was all about working hard, going to school and you'll be what you want to be. Going to college and getting involved in activism with Anti-coalition taught me that no, you can work as hard as you want to work and you can still end up in the gutter. Like you (Hannah Faye) said it is *Occupy the World* because in Italy there are two hundred thousand people getting mixed in with this whole situation. It's a direct message. We're not going to take it anymore. Half the people that are here are homeless. So if the protest hadn't been in Liberty Plaza it would've been somewhere else because the homeless situation is something that is not dealt with. We see them, we know that they're there, but if we can pretend they're not there then we'll do that. And when I say *us* or *we* I don't mean us, but the system as a whole. We live in a system that allows us to work, work, work but we don't see what we're working for. The corruption of Wall Street...for them to sit there and take trillions of our dollars...there are people who can't even think about trillion. That number is so massive. To them it's like what do you mean by *a trillion*? If we're sending 418 million dollars to Iraq a day that's money that could be used for community projects, senior citizen projects, and for education. Only 1-2% of the federal government's money goes to education for the whole country. But you (the government) can recruit young people to go fight in a war? They're not telling the truth about what's going on. There are people right now who hate *Occupy Wall Street* but they don't know anything about it. They've never been down here. They can't say there are good protesters or bad ones down here. No. They're (protesters) all good people. They're all using their voices and their bodies in the snow and rain to get the message out that we're not going to take this anymore. And we shouldn't take it anymore. In Oakland, California right now people are getting messed up because they want to occupy their community. I don't know the exact location where they want to occupy but they're calling it Oscar Grant Plaza. Oscar Grant was the man that was shot in the back by a policeman two years ago and it was all caught on tape. The policeman that shot him only got 11 months and he was released. In his (Oscar Grant's) honor and because of how massive the Occupy movement is the people decided to take it to that level. Now they're getting beat up by cops. Here...this was supposed to be a two month protest. But these protesters have been out here sleeping, forming their own community within the Liberty Plaza structure and they're getting beat up by cops too. It's like this, people who look like you are getting paid to hurt you. But all you're doing is using your voice to say enough is enough. This movement has the potential to be something massive. I'm 23 years old. I wasn't around during the 60's and 70's when the Panthers and all these groups were out doing their thing. But for me to be able to live through this...this is a big thing. I want to take the lessons that I learned from Malcolm X "by any means necessary" and what I believe in and build a community. I want to make sure that I learn something from being here, whether it be how to protect myself from police brutality or something else. On October 1st they arrested 700 people. That was a big deal. Actually I think that was one of the things that catapulted *Occupy Wall Street* to the front page because they really arrested 700 people on the bridge. They literally had people on the bridge for six hours. All people were trying to do was get from Liberty Park (Zucotti Park) to Camdan Plaza. That's it. And they arrested 700 people? They arrested people on a march that would've only taken thirty minutes to an hour. So I want to use what I've learned from being here and by talking to people to empower myself. My mother would never agree with me or come out for a demonstration. The thought of me even being here right now is probably making her shake in her old, little bones...poor thing. But I'm here to inform my community. Everything that I'm learning here...even by talking to you (Hannah Faye), being apart of Anti-coalition, every week I inform people about *Occupy Wall Street*. I inform people who don't know what's going on with the community struggle. The first week *Occupy Wall Street* began I wasn't a participant yet. But other people that I work with and know, like a friend of mine who's a conscious hip hop artist was there. He started telling me about what was going on and how things were setting up. I knew that I would have to come here eventually. I mean I was already doing work like this. So it was a given that I would have to be here. It's an obligation for me. I don't think people can call themselves conscious or an activist and ignore what's going on here. As an activist, you have to eventually make your way to these protests even if it's just to observe. Being on the fence is not going to do anything. It's not going to help. But it doesn't matter. Whether people come out here or not it's still going to keep moving. Occupy Wall Street has spread to Brooklyn, the Bronx, Queens, etc. If they can all pack up and get on the ferry they might go to Staten Island too (laughs). It's something that...whether or not you want to know about it it's there. It's there. People talk about it everyday. Another really big thing that happened was when they came and tried to clean up the park (Liberty Park). They said they needed everybody out of the park so they could "clean it up." Everybody was like *what*? Excuse me. No. We'll (the protesters) clean the park. It's okay. So then people were asking questions. It is a peaceful protest. Let these people (protesters) do what they have to do. It's not that serious. As this gets bigger and we see what's going on in Oakland and the world...there's even an *Occupy Kansas*. It's growing. It's going to keep growing and whether or not you want to be swallowed up pretty soon it's going to consume everything around you. You can't ignore it. If you don't want to be apart of the movement, go ahead because the majority of the people who are here are going to work very hard. We're the 99%. We need to come together in solidarity and collectively. If you're not about that then stay where you are. It's hard enough just to be here. It's freezing cold. They just gave them tents. They were just sleeping in sleeping bags on the ground. They have enough to deal with, with keeping their message alive. If you side with Fox News, if you side with the Post and with the Daily News and other media personnel that are only spreading negative gossip about what's going on here then you need to look into yourself and see what you're about. Whether you are for it or not for it, the truth is there. All these people have is the truth. And the truth is Wall Street is corrupt. People don't have homes. It's not because they don't work hard enough. It's not because they didn't try. It's because the government decided that giving them a place to live wasn't near as important as satisfying their own greed. That's obvious. We can't deny the money that we need is being used to occupy other nations. And you (the government) won't let people sit down in the park? It's going to continue whether or not people have something positive to say. It's excelling. It's because it's New York. It's the empire state and there's so much diversity here. I think being a young, black woman...23 years old and about to finish college and officially enter the world...one of the things that always sticks out to me is what Mumia Abu-Jamal said. He's on death row right now. He's been in prison since 1981. I think one of the most important things he ever said was: "It is dire that the youth take matters into their own hands." And it's true. A lot of times we meet older adults, not like your self Miss Hannah. But there are many adults who discourage us. They tell us not to go down there (Occupy Wall Street). We don't meet that many older adults who are like yes, I'll go with you! They try to deter us from building a consciousness about the world. Some of them think ignorance is bliss. They think it's easier to not know what's going on. It's easier to focus on the routine. It's harder to learn the truth and try to fight for it. They don't want fighters. As a young person I get to speak to other young people and tell them we need to be out here. Whether it's handing out flyers, like I do, whether it's coming down to see what's going on or if you just want to straight up, get a tent and occupy; even if it's doing something like what you're doing Miss Hannah and writing about this thing. It's important that we get involved. Another thing that Mumia said...it's kind of crazy though. When Obama was running for election people got really excited. There were people who cried who never thought they would live to see a black president. Historically, that was a big moment. But Mumia said: "Don't forget a politician's words are like a prostitute's kids. It's just business." So you can have someone that looks like you, but it doesn't necessarily mean they have your best interest at heart. But if we come together and make ourselves the people we look up to and fight for what we believe in...if we fight for what freedom really is and what justice and equality really are then we can fight for what our society *can* be. It's not just laws and voting for this person or that person. It's the spirit of organizing a community and building awareness. We can truly make something amazing that we won't be afraid to let our children live in. To people who call themselves revolutionists...Revolution starts with an *r*. So we have to change *our* selves and be open. Each one, teach one. Spread the message about Occupy Wall Street.

28

Student Revolutionary

Date: Saturday, October 29, 2011
Location: Wall Street, New York
Event: Occupy Wall Street
Occupation: Student
Age: 23
Transcribed Voice Recording

I am a participant in *Occupy Wall Street* because it has created a platform where all the demands and downfalls of what is called capitalism can be confronted. Capitalism is unrepresentative of the population that it's supposed to serve. It makes greed an acceptable attribute to society. It makes people view themselves as individuals instead of as a collective. It also leads us to build walls between each other because of race, color and ethnicity. These things alone do not make us human beings. At the end of the day, race does not determine whether or not you are a human being. Capitalism begins with prejudice because it is by race that one class is exploited over another. I am apart of two organizations. One of them is called the People Power Movement, which is basically community based and city funded. I'm also a member of Students United for a Free CUNY, which is a student movement in CUNY (City University of New York). We're demanding free tuition. In CUNY, it shows what racism has done. Tuition was free when the school was filled with predominantly white men. In 1963 they forecasted that by 1975 CUNY would be predominantly attended by people of color. It's not a coincidence that by 1976 tuition was actually implemented. Do you understand? Basically, they started filtering public higher education for people due to income and especially race. Race was a key factor in tuition being implemented at CUNY. History is the key. It basically shows you the path and it's going to give you the path to the future. We're part of history every single day because we're moving forward not backwards. I started reading. I started becoming more active, taking on roles in my community. I took on bigger roles in the student movements. And through this participation I started to realize most of the things that are going on in this country are products of racism. At the end of the day, you are categorized. You could even be considered in the working class and still be confronted with barriers especially in the bottom working class, where there are predominantly people of color. Do you understand? Growing up in Washington Heights, New York City...I experienced how it was being stopped by cops and frisked just because of my nationality and the assumption that I'm some type of criminal because of where I live. That basically fueled me with energy and with a voice to fight back. I know I'm not the only one who feels like this so now I help facilitate and encourage other people to stand up for their rights too. Occupy Wall Street is an open place for people to bring in their concerns. Hopefully our demands will be fulfilled through it. But as students united for a free CUNY, our demand is a free CUNY for everybody in New York City. Everybody that graduates from the public educational system in New York City should receive a free public higher education regardless of the color of their skin. This is why reading is so important. If you don't read you're basically going off of misconceptions and wrong theories. Do you understand? You have to be a critical thinker. Think for yourself. Read something, analyze it and don't criticize it because it's not about you. Take the things that are similar to something you're going through and try to connect it with your life. At the end of the day there's always going to be something misleading, but it doesn't mean it's entirely wrong. From those misconceptions you can learn how to improve things. Criticism is important. If you are open to criticism you are open to improvement. If you can't be criticized then I don't know how you can better yourself. I'm talking about bettering humanity at the same time too. We are here for the people who aren't here. We record everything for people who can't be physically here because we want people to be able to bring the message wherever they are. Just because you can't be here (Occupy Wall Street) and be apart of this...I mean, you're actually apart of it just by being alive. At the end of the day we're (protesters) fighting for better lives for people all over the world. Take this message into your communities and build from it. Know that you have somewhere you can go where a lot of people are congregating and speaking about their concerns and figuring out ways to fix it. Not being here shouldn't stop anyone from spreading the message and discussing issues that are important to them. The platform that is tumbling the giant is here. Any direction you might hit it from is acceptable. Occupy Wall Street just tumbled it. Now you choose where you want to hit it from. Without supporters it would be hard to move forward. We have to thank them for actually taking the time to give us resources because having resources is the key. The people are the ones that are funding us, not the government. We're being funded by the people and that's important. That shows that people are relating to us. They might not be able to be here but at the same time they're helping to facilitate and maintain us. I'm a human being. I try to respect everyone's thinking, but at the end of the day people who are thinking about us (protesters) as nothing but hippies don't understand that we're trying to find a solution. People who are against us are usually people that are comfortable. They are people who are profiting off of this empire. At the end of the day, I love it (sarcastically) when the news says "war is in the common interest of the American people." It is not in the common interest of the American people. It's in the common interest of corporations that profit from wars. American people lose lives. We lose lives from war. They (corporations) make money off of wars. We have to be clear on what side we stand. We stand for something and we will prevail. We will win. If not now, a hundred years from now, a thousand years from now...however many years it takes...a seed has been planted. It was planted through the Civil Rights Movement. It was planted through the Africans who survived slavery, the lynching and all the segregation. The strongest of us survived and we're still here. We're going to keep bringing it to the man. I also want to say it's not about going against one race of people because you have people like John Brown, who actually armed the Africans to fight against slavery in this country and he was white. People like him didn't support the inhumanities of slavery, regardless of being white or not. All of them ended up dying, but still they died for what they believed in and that's the idea. Regardless of the color of our skin, we are all human beings. Like Martin Luther King said, "An injustice here is an injustice everywhere." One form of injustice is an injustice all over the world. Do you understand? We have to stop thinking for ourselves and start thinking of people who are starving while we throw food away. This should not be a color thing. All of this stuff has been set up to stop us from unifying. At the end of the day we're all human beings. Everybody bleeds, everybody breaths, we all share the planet. Look past color, look beyond the walls that capitalism imposes. We're industrialized and we have all of this technology but at the expense of how many people? Be a human. We can't always compromise. We've been compromising (with the powers that be) for too long. Choose a side and stand by it. If you're going to be a human being, fight capitalism because it deprives us of our natural resources. It builds barriers amongst human beings. Do you understand? That's the message I want to get across. There's another saying that's similar to this one: it's not what your community can do for you, it's what you can do for your community. If our communities are experiencing hardships we shouldn't leave them behind, but be a strong voice within them, demanding for change. The new Bill of Rights was demanded by the people. When you think about it the government has never given the people anything. We've always had to fight for a change.

FINAL THOUGHT

What else is there to say? I can honestly say I'm proud to be a member of the 99%. I am proud to be a 99er. Collectively, we own more property and have more wealth and power than the 1%. For these reasons, I think the 1% should be considerate. If we (99) effectively ban together we have the power to change the world and make it a better place for ourselves and for our children. Imagine a place where no monetary system exists, but transactions are still being made decently and in order. Imagine a place where the color of your skin, your gender, your sexual orientation, your religion, your wealth or status, have nothing to do with your level of success. Imagine a place where the air is fresh and the food and water are both clean. A place where petroleum is no longer needed. A place where physicians and nurses wait on you without health insurance. A place where there is no lower, middle or upper class, but everyone is in the same class, focused on nothing else except for learning how to live in harmony with one another. Imagine living in a place where children don't spend as much time in school and yet they gain phenomenal knowledge. At the same time their parents don't have to spend as much time at work in order to put food on the table. Imagine living in a world where you are free to travel anywhere you would like at anytime without breaking your bank. Imagine a world where even the animals are given convenience. Imagine a world without the Federal Reserve. Imagine a world without so many people trying to lead at once. Imagine a world that embraced the naturally growing herbs and banned the artificial ones now growing in laboratories. Imagine if the politicians and government made it completely against the law to manufacture absolutely anything that was harmful to human life. Imagine if they eliminated jails and prisons and instead opened up counseling centers and places where criminals could really make a change. Imagine living in a world without taxes. Imagine living in a world where the leaders saw a need and simply met it. Imagine if every congress man and every congress woman declined an increase in their salaries. Imagine if every executive of every company shut down their businesses and sent everyone home. Imagine if fast food executives decided they were going to stop selling people poisonous foods. Imagine. Imagine if all of this was just the beginning. Now I ask: What is your occupation?

Occupy the World: From the Heart of the Protesters

By Hannah Faye

What are your feelings? Are you a participant or non-participant in the Occupy Movement? Want to share your thoughts? Visit arapperscollege.weebly.com today and add your own feelings along with your location to the blog entitled: *Occupy the World: From the Heart of the Protesters*. Keeping your comments insightful will ensure their survival on my site. There are plenty of blog lawns for dog shit. Mine isn't one of them. Peace. :)